# Preface

This report is designed to help readers better understand some of the basic facts related to the diminished life chances for boys and men of color in California. By examining the differences in relative odds for different outcomes, we provide evidence of the link between poor outcomes in specific areas and diminished life chances for boys and young men of color. Progress on improving the odds for boys and men of color in California begins with a common understanding of what the biggest challenges are and what we know about how to start addressing those challenges.

This report provides a broad overview of areas where the greatest disparities for boys and men of color exist as a way to identify possible starting points for addressing these disparities. In particular, we worked with The California Endowment to identify four broad outcome domains and select specific indicators within each domain to examine where boys and young men of color now stand relative to their white counterparts. Despite the high odds working against boys and men of color, there is reason for hope, as there are significant areas of opportunity in which to begin making an important difference in changing the life course of boys and men of color. We present information about different strategies for diminishing the disparities for boys and men of color, including effective programs, practices and policies.

In this report, we highlight those indicators in which the likelihoods for certain social outcomes— for example, being born to a teenage mother, being the victim of homicide, or not completing high school—are two times greater than they are for white boys and men, showing the data behind the odds and briefly discussing some of the possible causes and consequences of the poor outcomes we find. In the appendix, we provide the detailed results for the indicators for which the disparities between boys and men of color are not as great.

These results will be of interest to The California Endowment and other foundations, as well as to policymakers, community leaders, and others responsible for improving the well-being of California's children and ensuring collaboration between key stakeholders at the state and local levels to address these issues.

This work was prepared for The California Endowment and produced within the RAND Health Promotion and Disease Prevention Program (HPDP). RAND HPDP is a division of RAND Health and addresses issues related to measuring healthy and unhealthy behaviors, examining the distribution of health behaviors across population subgroups, identifying what causes or influences such behaviors, and designing and evaluating interventions to improve health behaviors. Information about RAND Health and its research and publications can be found at http://www.rand.org/health/. Visit The California Endowment website at http://www.calendow.org.

# Contents

Tables    4

Figures    6

Summary    10

     Boys and Men of Color in California    10
     A Standard Metric for Capturing Disparities    10
     Disparities in a Social Determinant Context    11
     The Findings    13
       *Socioeconomic Disparities*    13
       *Health Disparities*    14
       *Safety Disparities*    16
       *Ready to Learn Disparities*    16
     Reducing the Disparities    19
       *What The California Endowment Is Doing*    24
     Conclusions    25

Acknowledgments    27

Abbreviations    28

CHAPTER 1: Introduction    30
     A Standard Metric for Capturing Disparities    32
     What Lies Ahead    33

CHAPTER 2: Disparities in a Social Determinant Context    36
     Grounding our Analysis – A Conceptual Framework    36
     Overview of California Demographics    38

CHAPTER 3: Assessing Disparities Faced by Boys and Men of Color in California    40
     Socioeconomic Disparities    42
       *Children Living in Poverty*    42
       *Maternal Education (Less Than High School)*    43
       *Children in Single-Parent Households*    44
       *Children with Unemployed Parents*    45
     Health Disparities    45
       *Low Birth Weight*    45
       *Births to Unmarried Women*    47
       *Births to Teen Mothers*    48
       *Infant Mortality*    49
       *Childhood Asthma*    50
       *Childhood Obesity*    50
       *Post-Traumatic Stress Disorder*    51
       *Health Insurance*    52
       *Access to Health Care*    53
       *HIV and AIDS*    53

Safety                                                                           54
    *Witnessing Domestic Violence and Exposure to*
      *Other Forms of Violence*                                     55
    *Substantiated Child Abuse and Neglect*                           55
    *Foster Care*                                                     57
    *Juvenile Arrest and Custody Rates*                               57
    *Lifetime Likelihood of Ever Going to Prison*                     58
    *Disproportional Representation in the Prison Population*          59
    *Incarceration Rate*                                              59
    *Children with Incarcerated Parents*                              60
    *Firearms-Related Death Rates*                                    61
    *Homicide-Related Death Rates*                                    62
Ready to Learn                                                                   62
    *High School Completion*                                          63
    *Student Achievement: Math and Reading Proficiency*               63
    *School Suspension*                                               64
    *Grade Retention*                                                 65
Geographic Concentration of Disadvantage:
    Neighborhood Effects                                              66

CHAPTER 4:  Addressing Disparities Faced by
               Boys and Men of Color in California                   70
Reducing the Disparities: The Macro Level                                        71
Reducing the Disparities: The Community Level                                    72
Reducing the Disparities: The Interpersonal and Individual Levels                75
    *What The California Endowment Is Doing*                           79
Summary                                                                          85

CHAPTER 5:  Conclusions                                                          86

Appendix:  Summary of Other Outcome Indicators                                   92
Socioeconomic                                                                    92
    *Youth Unemployment*                                              93
Health                                                                           93
    *Childhood Asthma*                                                93
    *Social and Emotional Well-Being*                                 93
    *Alcohol and Substance Use*                                       95
    *Access to Health Care*                                           97
    *Sexually Transmitted Diseases*                                  101
Safety                                                                          102
    *Three Strikes Conviction*                                       103
    *Witnessing Domestic Violence*                                   105
    *Exposure to Other Forms of Violence*                            105
    *Witnessing Violence/Indirect Victimization*                     107
Ready to Learn                                                                  108
    *Absenteeism*                                                    110
    *Enrollment in Preschool or Pre-K*                               111

References                                                                      112

# Tables

Table S.1    The Underlying Conceptual Framework    12

Table S.2    Socioeconomic Disparities: Odds for Boys and Men of Color Relative to White Boys and Men    13

Table S.3    Health Disparities: Odds for Boys and Men of Color Relative to White Boys and Men    15

Table S.4    Safety Disparities: Odds for Boys and Men of Color Relative to White Boys and Men    17

Table S.5    Ready to Learn Disparities: Odds for Boys and Men of Color Relative to White Boys and Men    19

Table 2.1    Macro, Community and Interpersonal Context of Individual Well-Being    37

Table 3.1    Socioeconomic Outcome Indicators with Odds for Boys and Men of Color Greater Than Twice What They Are for White Boys and Men    42

Table 3.2    Health Outcome Indicators with Odds for Boys and Men of Color Greater Than Twice What They Are for White Boys and Men    46

Table 3.3    Safety Outcome Indicators with Odds for Boys and Men of Color Greater Than Twice What They Are for White Boys and Men    54

Table 3.4    Ready to Learn Outcome Indicators with Odds for Boys and Men of Color Greater Than Twice What They Are for White Boys and Men    62

Table 4.1    Examples of Indicators and Number of Programs Listed on Promising Practices Network Website    76

Table A.1    Odds Relative to Whites by Race/Ethnicity for Socioeconomic Indicators    93

Table A.2    Odds Relative to Whites by Race/Ethnicity
             for Health Indicators                                    94

Table A.3    Sexually Transmitted Disease Rates
             (per 100,000 Adult Males Ages 20 to 24)                 103

Table A.4    Odds Relative to Whites by Race/Ethnicity
             for Safety Indicators                                   104

Table A.5    Second and Third Strikers Males in the
             Adult Institution Population by Race/Ethnicity,
             as of December 31, 2007                                 106

Table A.6    Violent and Property Victimization by Race
             of Victim or Race of Head of Household, 2006            108

Table A.7    Rate of Witnessing or Indirect Victimization
             (per 1,000 Children)                                    109

Table A.8    Odds Relative to Whites by Race/Ethnicity
             for Ready to Learn Indicators                           110

# Figures

Figure 2.1    Percent Distribution by Age and by Race and Hispanic Origin, California and the U.S., 2006    38

Figure 3.1    Children Living in Poverty    43

Figure 3.2    Mothers With No High School Degree    44

Figure 3.3    Single-Parent Families    45

Figure 3.4    Unemployed Parents    46

Figure 3.5    Low Birth Weight Infants    47

Figure 3.6    Births to Unmarried Women    48

Figure 3.7    Births to Teen Mothers    49

Figure 3.8    Infant Mortality    50

Figure 3.9    Children's Hospitalization for Asthma    51

Figure 3.10    Childhood Obesity    51

Figure 3.11    Adolescent Post-Traumatic Stress Disorder    52

Figure 3.12    Uninsured Children    53

Figure 3.13    Children Without a Usual Source of Medical Care    53

Figure 3.14    HIV and AIDS    54

Figure 3.15    Children's Witnessing of Domestic Violence and Exposure to Other Forms of Violence    55

Figure 3.16    Child Abuse and Neglect    56

Figure 3.17    Children in Foster Care    57

Figure 3.18    Juvenile Arrest Rates    58

Figure 3.19    Custody Rates    58

Figure 3.20   Lifetime Likelihood of Going to Prison                    59

Figure 3.21   Disproportionality Index for Prison Population            60

Figure 3.22   Incarceration Rate                                        60

Figure 3.23   Children with Incarcerated Parents                        61

Figure 3.24   Firearms-Related Death Rate                               61

Figure 3.25   Homicide-Related Death Rate                               62

Figure 3.26   No High School Degree                                     63

Figure 3.27   Below Proficiency on Reading Test                         64

Figure 3.28   Below Proficiency on Math Test                            64

Figure 3.29   School Suspension                                         65

Figure 3.30   Grade Retention                                           65

Figure A.1    Unemployment Rate for 20-24 Year-Olds, by
              Gender and Race/Hispanic Origin (percent)                 93

Figure A.2    Prevalence of Active Asthma by Race/Ethnicity,
              California 2003 (percent)                                 95

Figure A.3    Percent of Children (Age 0-17) With at Least
              One Emergency Department Visit for Asthma
              by Race/Ethnicity Among Those With Active
              Asthma, California 2003                                   96

Figure A.4    Percent of Children (Age 5-11) Who Missed
              at Least 1 Day of School Due to Asthma Among
              Those With Active Asthma, California 2003                  96

Figure A.5    Percent of Adolescents (Age 12-17) in California
              in 2005 Who Ever Felt Depressed in Past 7 days and
              Who Ever Felt Sad in Past 7 days, by Race/Ethnicity        97

Figure A.6    Percent of 12-20 Year-Olds Who Drank in the Past
              30 Days, by Gender and Race/Hispanic Origin              98

Figure A.7    Percent of Adolescents 12-17 Who Ever Had
              a Few Sips of Alcohol in the Past Month, by
              Gender and Race/Hispanic Origin                          99

Figure A.8    Percent of 12-20 Year-Olds Who Reported *Binge*
              Drinking in the Past 30 Days, by Gender and
              Race/Hispanic Origin                                     99

Figure A.9    Percent of Adolescents 12-17 in California Who
              Reported *Binge* Drinking in the Past Month, by
              Race/Hispanic Origin                                     100

Figure A.10   Percent of High School Students Who Had Ever
              Used Cocaine or Ever Used Heroin, by
              Race/Hispanic Origin                                     100

Figure A.11   Percent of Adolescents 12-17 Who Currently
              Smoke, by Gender and Race/Hispanic Origin                101

Figure A.12   Emergency Room Visits in the Past 12 Months,
              Children and Adolescents, California 2003                102

Figure A.13   Average Annual Rate (2001-2005) of Nonfatal
              Intimate Partner Victimization per 1,000 Persons
              Age 12 or Older, by Gender and Race                      107

Figure A.14   Rate of Intimate Partner Homicide Victimization
              per 100,000 Adults in California, by Race/Ethnicity      108

"... neighborhood social cohesion, family, social support and parent education are also important contributors to an individual's development and well-being."

# Summary

## Boys and Men of Color in California

An expanding body of literature has documented that racial and ethnic disparities exist across a broad array of domains (Williams and Collins, 1995; Krieger et al., 1993). The literature also addresses how racial and ethnic disparities have developed and persisted over time in the context of historical and structural racism that has shaped policies, practices, and programs in ways that create disadvantage for certain groups (Aspen Institute Roundtable on Community Change, 2004; Hofrichter, 2003). This history and institutionalization of disadvantage has meant that "inequities that exist at all levels of society have persistent, profound, and long-lasting effects" (King County Equity and Social Justice Initiative, 2008). Within this context, boys and men of color are particularly vulnerable. The literature has found that inequities exist for boys and men of color across multiple domains. For example, boys and men of color have lower high school graduation rates, a greater likelihood of going to prison, and higher mortality rates from homicide (Dellums Commission, 2006).

Given that many of the inequities are especially great for boys and men of color, The California Endowment commissioned this report to examine and document racial and ethnic disparities for boys and men of color in California. This report provides detailed information on areas where the greatest disparities for boys and men of color exist identifying possible starting points for addressing these disparities. We worked with The California Endowment to identify four broad outcome domains—socioeconomic, health, safety, and ready to learn—and to select specific indicators within each domain from a range of possibilities. We then analyzed available data to quantify the magnitude of the disparities.

## A Standard Metric for Capturing Disparities

For each indicator in each of the chosen outcome domains, we use a standard method for comparing the data and measuring the disparities. This method involves calculating the "odds" for boys and men of color—in this case, Latino and African-American boys and men—compared with white boys and men. What are the odds, for example, that an African-American or Latino boy will be arrested relative to a white boy, and how great is the disparity? By expressing the disparities in terms of odds, we provide a simple way to quantify the increased risk of one group over another. If one group has higher odds than another, then that means there is a disparity between the groups for that indicator. We calculated the odds by dividing the rate or percentage for boys and men of color by the rate or percentage for white boys and young men. While any disproportion in odds is a concern, we focus on those indicators where the odds are *two times greater or more* for boys and men of color relative to their white peers. Specifically, we report on those indicators for which at least one of the groups (Latinos or African Americans) met the threshold of 2.0 higher odds than whites. Although this cut-off point is somewhat arbitrary, we believe that it serves as a useful starting point to help policymakers prioritize policy actions. Whenever possible, we provide male-only statistics, in keeping with the intent of The California Endowment. However, for some indicators, data by gender are simply not available. Likewise, we provide the odds for California only, unless only national data are available. In cases where such national data are available and where the differences provide a meaningful contrast, we compare California with the rest of the nation.

## Disparities in a Social Determinant Context

In trying to understand where disparities come from and how to address them, we grounded our research in the context of a conceptual framework based on the Northridge, Sclar, and Biswas (2003) model, which describes the contextual factors that interact to promote or inhibit individual health outcomes. This model highlights the multiple pathways by which factors in the physical, social, economic, and family domains contribute to individual well-being. We modified their framework to include safety and education (or ready to learn) outcomes at the individual level. See **Table S.1**. A more detailed version of the framework is provided in Chapter Two of this report.

At the macro level, social factors, such as cultural institutions, economic and political systems and ideologies, interact with inequalities in wealth, employment and educational opportunities and political influence. These inequalities, in turn, also influence the social context in which a child develops. At the community level, the built environment includes such factors as land use, availability of services and transportation, recreational resources (such as parks), and the type of housing and schools available. A community's social context takes into account the quality of education, local policies, political influence and the amount of community investment. At the micro/interpersonal level, stressors can include such factors as violent crime, unsafe housing, financial insecurity and unfair treatment. In terms of social support and family assets, neighborhood social cohesion, family, social support, and parent education are also important contributors to an individual's development and well-being. In addition, individual health behaviors, including substance use, dietary practices, and physical activity, also are important influences on outcomes.

Three key aspects of this framework are important in considering the results we present. First, individual outcomes and behavior are not generated in isolation but rather are embedded in a social and economic environment. Second, the individual-level outcomes are likely to be related, because they are produced in the same underlying context. Third, this framework captures the complex set of factors that contribute to disparities in the odds for boys and young men of color.

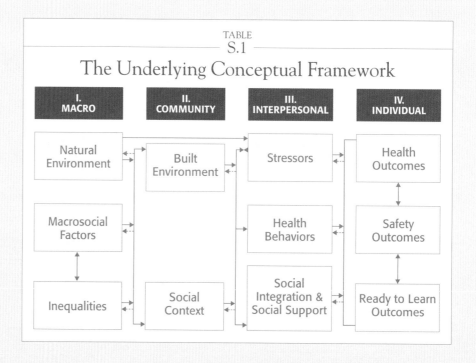

TABLE
S.1

## The Underlying Conceptual Framework

# The Findings

For the four sets of outcomes, we find that the odds for boys and men of color are far worse (more than two times worse) than they are for white boys and men across a number of indicators. In the following sections, we present those indicators within each of the outcome areas, and in each table we highlight in grey the outcomes for which the results are two times worse, or greater, for either Latinos or African Americans. Below, we highlight indicators with some of the largest disparities within each outcome area.

## Socioeconomic Disparities

California has experienced higher child poverty rates than the country as a whole since the early 1980s. Between 2002 and 2005, the child poverty rate remained about 19 percent overall. African-American and Latino children in California experience the highest rates of child poverty—each at about 27 percent. As **Table S.2** shows, African-American and Latino children are 3.4 times more likely than white children to live in poverty. California poverty rates are associated with family structure, parental education and parental work status. Families with a single mother have the highest poverty rates, at 42 percent, while married-couple families have a rate of only 12 percent. About half of the poor children in California live in families in which neither parent finished high school; the rate of poverty in these families is 44 percent (Public Policy Institute of California, 2006).

TABLE
S.2

## Socioeconomic Disparities

Odds for Boys and Men of Color Relative to White Boys and Men

| Indicator | Latino | African-American |
|---|---|---|
| Children living in poverty | 3.4 | 3.4 |
| Maternal education (less than high school) | 10.2 | 2.0 |
| Children in single-parent households | 1.1 | 2.5 |
| Children living with unemployed parents | 1.6 | 2.4 |

In terms of maternal education, white and African-American mothers in California tend to be more educated than their counterparts in the rest of the United States, but this advantage is not as great for Latino mothers. In California, African-American mothers are two times more likely than white mothers to have less than a high school education, while Latino mothers are more than ten times more likely than white mothers to have less than a high school education (**Table S.2**). Several decades of research have demonstrated strong links between maternal education and a range of child outcomes (Coleman et al., 1966; Leibowitz, 1977; McLanahan, 2004; Carneiro, Meghir, and Parey, 2007). Such research has argued that maternal education may improve children's well-being, both because maternal education is highly correlated with other socioeconomic determinants of children's outcomes—such as family income and neighborhood quality—and also because maternal education is associated with better caregiving, resulting in better health practices, home literacy, and other behaviors that promote child development (Desai and Alva, 1998).

## Health Disparities

**Table S.3** shows that, in the area of health, the odds of an infant being born to a teenage mother in California are 3.6 times greater for Latino infants than for white infants. African-American infants are more than twice as likely as white infants to be born to a teenage mother. Children that are born to teenage mothers have a greater chance of repeating a grade, dropping out of high school and being unemployed as young adults. Many of the risk factors for teenage pregnancy are related to socioeconomic status. Poverty, low education level and lack of employment are all predictors of pregnancy for teenagers of all racial and ethnic groups.

Nationally, 9 percent of children 18 years of age or younger have active asthma, compared with 8.6 percent of children under age 18 in California (Bloom and Cohen, 2007; California Department of Health Services, 2007). In California, the odds of having active asthma are 1.7 times higher for African-American children than they are for white children; in addition, 7 percent of Latino children have active asthma (Meng et al., 2007). Disproportionality in asthma burden among California children can be measured by differences in hospitalization rates. As **Table S.3** shows, African-American male children have asthma hospitalization rates 3.7 times greater than their white counterparts. Risk factors for asthma include living in an urban area (especially the inner city), which may increase exposure to environmental pollutants; substandard housing; respiratory infections in childhood; low birth weight; obesity; having one or both parents with asthma; and exposure to secondhand smoke (Mayo Clinic, 2008; California Department of Health Services, 2007).

Nationally, the risk of contracting HIV or AIDS is 6.9 times higher for African-American male adults and adolescents than for whites (**Table S.3**). Latinos are 3.1 times more likely than whites to have HIV or AIDS. HIV works against the immune system and allows infections to grow and spread throughout the body; it is most commonly transmitted through sexual contact and injection drug use. In California, HIV-related mortality is the

TABLE
S.3

## Health Disparities

Odds for Boys and Men of Color Relative to White Boys and Men

| Indicator | Latino | African-American |
|---|---|---|
| Very low birth weight | 1.0 | 2.6 |
| Births to unmarried women | 2.2 | 3.0 |
| Births to teen mothers | 3.6 | 2.2 |
| Infant mortality | 1.2 | 2.8 |
| Childhood asthma hospitalizations | 1.1 | 3.7 |
| Childhood obesity | 2.0 | 0.8 |
| Post-Traumatic Stress Disorder (PTSD) | 4.1 | 2.5 |
| Health insurance (lack of) (0-17 years) | 4.8 | 0.6 |
| Access to health care (no usual source of care) (0-11 years) | 2.5 | 1.1 |
| HIV and AIDS | 3.1 | 6.9 |

eighth-leading cause of death for African-American men and the tenth-leading cause for Latino men (Lee and McConville, 2007).

## Safety Disparities

In the area of safety, **Table S.4** shows that, for most of the indicators, the magnitude of the increased odds is highest for African Americans. Nationally, African-American men are 5.5 times more likely than white men to go to prison in their lifetime, and the odds for Latino men for this outcome are 2.9 times higher than for white men. Overall, 1 in 3 African-American men, 1 in 6 Latino men, and 1 in 17 white men are expected to go to prison during their lifetime (assuming current trends in incarceration rates) (Bonczar, 2003). Changes in first incarceration and mortality rates between 1974 and 2001 have had different impacts on lifetime incarceration depending on race and ethnicity. The likelihood of African American men going to prison over their lifetimes has increased more than any other group, with Latino men experiencing the second-largest increase. Based on current rates of first incarceration, an estimated 6.7 percent of African-American men in the United States will enter state or federal prison by age 20, compared with 3 percent of Latino men and less than 1 percent of white men (Bonczar, 2003).

Nationally, African-American children are almost 9 times more likely, and Latino children are more than 3 times more likely than white children to have a parent in prison (**Table S.4**). An estimated 856,000 California children—approximately 1 in 9—have a parent currently involved in the adult criminal justice system (Simmons, 2000).[1] The imprisonment of parents disrupts parent-child relationships, alters the networks of familial support, and places new burdens on governmental services, such as schools, foster care, adoption agencies and youth-serving organizations (Travis, McBride, and Solomon, 2005). Children of incarcerated parents are more likely to exhibit low self-esteem, depression, emotional withdrawal from friends and family, and inappropriate or disruptive behavior at home and in school, and they are at increased risk of future delinquency and criminal behavior (Travis and Waul, 2003).

[1]  *Calculation of 1 in 9 children is based on U.S. Census Bureau March 1999 Current Population Survey. There were about 9.8 million children ages 0–18 in California in 1999 (Simmons, 2000).*

Some of the greatest disparities we observed are for African Americans' homicide-related death rates. Homicide is the sixth-leading cause of death among African-American men and the seventh-leading cause of death among Latino men in California (Lee and McConville, 2007).[2] Young African-American men (15–24 years) have a homicide death rate at least 16 times greater than that of young white men (**Table S.4**), and young Latino men have a homicide death rate 5 times greater than that of young white men. In addition, African Americans and Latinos have increased odds relative to whites of being exposed to other forms of violence, such as shootings, bombs or riots.

TABLE
S.4

## Safety Disparities

Odds for Boys and Men of Color Relative to White Boys and Men

| Indicator | Latino | African-American |
|---|---|---|
| Witnessing domestic violence | 1.1 | 2.1 |
| Exposure to other forms of violence (shootings, bombs, or riots) | 2.1 | 3.0 |
| Substantiated child abuse and neglect | 1.3 | 2.5 |
| Disproportional representation in foster care* | .89 | 4.05 |
| Lifetime likelihood of ever going to prison | 2.9 | 5.5 |
| Disproportional representation in prison population* | 1.07 | 4.3 |
| Incarceration rate | 1.5 | 6.7 |
| Children with incarcerated parents | 3.3 | 8.8 |
| Juvenile arrest rate | 1.2 | 2.5 |
| Juvenile custody rate | 2.1 | 5.7 |
| Firearms-related death rate | 3.3 | 10.1 |
| Homicide-related death rate | 5.1 | 16.4 |

* This is not an odds ratio, but rather it is a disproportionality index number. For foster care, the index represents the proportion of children in the foster care system compared with that group's overall proportion in the general population. An index number below 1.00 indicates an underrepresentation in foster care compared with the proportion in the general child population, while a number above 1.00 indicates an overrepresentation of children in foster care. For the prison population, the index represents the proportion of African-Americans or Latinos in the prison population compared with each group's overall proportion in the general population. An index number above 1.00 indicates an overrepresentation in the prison population.

---

2  For adult African-American men (25 years and older), heart disease drives much of the mortality disadvantage, followed by homicide. The time period for the death certificate data is 2000–2002.

In California, African-American children are overrepresented in foster care, with a disproportionality index of 4.05 (**Table S.4**). This index represents the proportion of children in the foster care system compared with that group's overall proportion in the general population. An index number above 1.00 indicates an overrepresentation of children in foster care compared with that group's proportion in the general child population. Children are removed from their home and placed in foster care when they cannot be adequately protected from maltreatment. Maltreated children are more likely to be depressed, abuse alcohol or drugs, engage in risky sexual behavior, perform poorly in school and become involved with the criminal justice system. The risk factors for child maltreatment include such parent, family and community characteristics as poverty, unemployment, teen parents and alcohol or drug use.

### Ready to Learn Disparities

In the ready to learn area (**Table S.5**), the increased odds for Latinos and African Americans are comparable and focused within the achievement and proficiency indicators. African-American Californians over age 25 are nearly twice as likely to be without a high school diploma as whites, while Latinos in California are almost seven times as likely to be without a high school degree (**Table S.5**). This extremely large gap for Latinos is explained in part by the differences in educational attainment between native-born and other residents. In California, about nine out of ten native-born U.S. citizens have a high school degree, compared with only half of noncitizens and three-quarters of naturalized citizens (California Department of Finance, 2007b). In addition to accounting for earnings differences, high school graduation status is also linked to improvements in other outcomes, such as health status (Smith, 2005) and children's outcomes (Currie and Morretti, 2003).

In California, both Latino and African-American children are at increased risk for being below basic proficiency in math and in reading. For both African-American and Latino students, the gaps between their scores and those of whites are larger for math than for reading. These gaps shrink between fourth grade and eighth grade for math, but for reading, they grow slightly for African Americans and stay the same for Latinos. California children perform below the national average on most measures of academic achievement. One way that California differs from the rest of the country is that in the grade 4 tests, Latinos are the most likely to score below basic proficiency, while in the rest of the country African Americans are most likely to score below basic proficiency. However, for the grade 8 tests, the race and ethnicity patterns in California mirror those in the rest of the nation, with African Americans being the most likely to score below basic proficiency.

TABLE
S.5

## Ready to Learn Disparities

Odds for Boys and Men of Color Relative to White Boys and Men

| Indicator | Latino | African-American |
|---|---|---|
| High school noncompletion | 6.7 | 1.9 |
| Student achievement: below reading proficiency (grade 4) | 2.3 | 2.2 |
| Student achievement: below reading proficiency (grade 8) | 2.3 | 2.4 |
| Student achievement: below math proficiency (grade 4) | 3.6 | 3.5 |
| Student achievement: below math proficiency (grade 8) | 2.5 | 2.8 |
| School suspension | 1.2 | 2.4 |
| Grade retention | 1.1 | 2.0 |

## Reducing the Disparities

The conceptual framework in **Table S.1** illustrates that there are multiple pathways through which factors in the physical, social, economic, and family domains contribute to individual well-being. A growing body of research suggests that the disparities in odds for boys and men of color that we summarize here are largely the result of a cumulative set of factors—including adverse socioeconomic conditions and unequal access to health care, quality education, adequate housing and employment—which, together, play large roles in generating these disparities. Given this broader context, what can policymakers, government agencies, philanthropic foundations, community organizations and service providers do to improve the life chances of boys and men of color in California?

Within this framework of macro-, community, and interpersonal/individual-level factors, national organizations, such as the National Urban League, the Joint Center for Political and Economic Studies, and the Congressional Hispanic Caucus—as well as foundations such as the W.K. Kellogg Foundation and the Ford Foundation—have made major contributions to understanding disparities among racial and ethnic groups and developing an action agenda for addressing these inequalities. The 2006 Dellums Commission report (Dellums Commission, 2006) undertook a comprehensive examination of a range of policies that limit the life chances of young men of color and their communities, and made a number of recommendations for policy change. Collectively, this body of work has led to important steps at the national level, such as federal legislation to establish an Office of Men's Health within the Department of Health and Human Services (DHHS) to examine the social determinants of health.

**At the macro level**, the recommendations from various commissions and expert panels often stress identifying and addressing inequities in the systems that provide employment, educational or service opportunities. For example, one policy-level approach for addressing factors that contribute to disparities in foster care is in the area of legal guardianship. In its report, *African American Children in Foster Care* (2007), The U.S. Government Accountability Office (GAO) recommended that Congress consider amending federal law to allow federal reimbursement for legal guardianship in much the same way as it is currently done for adoption. This would assist states in increasing the number of homes available for the permanent placement of African-American and other children out of foster care. To enhance states' ability to reduce the proportion of African-American children in foster care, the GAO also recommended that the Secretary of Health and Human Services help states understand the nature and extent of disproportionality in their child welfare systems by, for example, encouraging states to regularly track state and local data on the ethnic and racial disproportionality of children in foster care.

Prisoner reentry is another area where policy-level approaches can help improve links between communities and state systems and data analysis can be used for identifying opportunities for improvement. The California Department of Corrections and Rehabilitation (CDCR) Expert Panel, in its *Report to the California State Legislature: A Roadmap for Effective Offender Programming* (CDCR, 2007b), put forth a set of recommendations for improving programming, the parole system, and reentry resources to help in transitioning ex-offenders back into the community. One key recommendation was that the CDCR develop and strengthen its formal partnerships with community stakeholders on reentry, including establishing interagency steering committees at the community and state levels to coordinate the transition of services for those returning from prison back to their communities.

**At the community level**, more opportunities exist to make changes that are likely to reduce the disparities for boys and men of color. For example, in 1994, Multnomah County, Oregon, addressed the problem of youth of color being disproportionately represented in its juvenile system by implementing a series of reforms that included establishing a Disproportionate Minority Confinement Committee that relied on objective analysis of data to achieve racial parity by 2000 (Dellums Commission, 2006).

The public health community has increasingly recognized "social determinants" of health as primary predictors of individual outcomes. Community-level factors include access to *health-promoting* services, such as parks, or to *health-robbing* experiences, such as relentless community violence, exposure to environmental toxins and poor school quality. Actions to improve community-level factors that can improve the odds for boys and men of color encompass a vast spectrum of activities and may use a variety of strategies to address numerous challenges. For instance, zoning laws can have an impact both on access to services and on reducing harmful environmental exposures. In Los Angeles County, the Child Care Planning Committee and the Policy Roundtable on Child Care worked to modify zoning laws so that more children of color will have access to licensed child care settings. To address disparities in environmental exposure, Washington, D.C. lawmakers undertook pollution-reduction measures, such as enforcing anti-idling ordinances and regulating small-source emissions, and announced reductions in the number of unhealthy air quality days in the District by nearly half (District of Columbia Department of the Environment, 2006). The District had the highest rates of asthma in the country, and reducing unhealthy air quality days was expected to improve asthma outcomes for children, most of whom are children of color (District of Columbia Department of Health, 2000).

Community partnerships – which involve mobilizing resources across community institutions in a coordinated effort to address a particular issue – are increasingly recognized as a promising community-level approach to addressing complex social problems, such as racial disparities, that have multifaceted causes and cross the boundaries of any one organization. The advantages of community partnerships may include increased efficiency gained by eliminating duplicated services, improved service coordination and integration, and modification of community norms and values to promote healthy behaviors. One example of a comprehensive community initiative is the Ford Foundation's Neighborhood and Family Initiative. Implemented in four cities over a five-year period, the initiative sought to develop and integrate social, physical and economic efforts throughout the community, with a strong focus on community involvement in the change process (Chaskin et al., 2001).

**At the interpersonal and individual levels**, the most proximate approach generally taken to improve outcomes is to implement "programs," which operate by changing the intra- and interpersonal factors that affect individual outcomes. One example of a program with a strong evidence base is Cognitive-Behavioral Intervention for Trauma in Schools (CBITS)—a school-based intervention to help children traumatized by violence. In Los Angeles, public middle schools with mostly Latino students received CBITS from school-based mental health clinicians. Students from economically disadvantaged neighborhoods who participated in the program were found to have significantly fewer symptoms of post-traumatic stress, depression and psychosocial dysfunction (Jaycox et al., 2002). Extending the CBITS program to other disadvantaged communities within California may help improve the emotional well-being of boys and young men of color and reduce some of the disparities in this area.

Implementing evidence-based "model programs" is not always practical, because communities vary in their resources, needs and cultural context, As a result, many individual-level interventions adapt the practices of model programs to their own context. Practices are more difficult to evaluate, because there is less information in the scientific literature on which to base effective practice guidelines. Examples of the types of practices widely represented in effective approaches for improving outcomes for children and youth include mentoring, the infusion of behavioral health services, comprehensive or integrative services and learning using non-didactic approaches:

- **Mentoring**. More than a dozen programs listed on the Promising Practices Network (PPN)—a collaboration between the RAND Corporation and public and private organizations to systematically review scientific evidence related to improving outcomes for children and families – use mentoring as one of the primary practices in improving outcomes for young people. From massive nationwide programs to small-scale model ones, programs built around mentoring have been shown to increase the number of youths graduating from high school, reduce conduct problems, improve performance on measures of achievement, and improve other indicators highlighted above. Evidence-based mentoring programs operating in California include Big Brothers/Big Sisters, Achievement for Latinos Through Academic Success, and Multi-Dimensional Treatment Foster Care.

- **Infusion of Behavioral Health Services**. Many of the effective approaches to improving the well-being of young people recognize the need to couple services that target a particular outcome and behavioral health services. For example, programs that are specifically designed to target substance abuse, gang involvement, or violence prevention are increasingly likely to include components to address behavioral health issues, including post-traumatic stress, anxiety and depression. The CBITS program is one example. Another example is Multisystemic Therapy (MST), an intensive, family-based treatment approach for improving the behavior of serious juvenile offenders (Curtis, Ronan, and Borduin, 2004).

- **Comprehensive or Integrated Services**. Another hallmark of many approaches is the emphasis on services that cut across outcome areas or bureaucratic functional lines. For example, early childhood intervention services are most often provided using a combination of preschool, home visiting, early screening and case management, rather than one of these alone (Karoly, Kilburn, and Cannon, 2005). An example from the field of juvenile justice is providing wraparound case management services designed to keep delinquent youth at home and out of institutions, where possible. In California, the Repeat Offender Prevention Program (ROPP) (a demonstration program from 1996 to 2002) provided wraparound services to at-risk youth (ages 8 to 15 years), including first-time offenders, youth with chronic truancy problems and gang-involved and substance-abusing youth (California Board of Corrections, 2002).

- **Learning Using Non-Didactic Approaches**. A final example of a practice that is represented among many of the effective program models is the recognition that participant learning should take place through experiential approaches, such as role-playing, rather than through didactic approaches, such as straight lecturing. Examples of this come from the substance-abuse prevention arena, where California interventions, such as *Keepin' It R.E.A.L.* (Promising Practices Network, 2008c) and *Project ALERT* (Promising Practices Network, 2008d), focus on practicing resistance skills, learning the benefits of not using alcohol, tobacco, and other drugs, and recognizing that most people do not use drugs.

## What The California Endowment Is Doing

Some other examples of practices in these four areas include ongoing programs funded by The California Endowment that address some of the health and safety issues identified above for boys and men of color. They are summarized on the following page.

# Conclusions

In this report, we highlight a number of disparities in four outcome areas: socioeconomic, health, safety, and ready to learn. Although there are large odds working against boys and men of color, there is a growing body of research that identifies approaches at the macro, community, interpersonal and individual levels that can improve those odds. Interventions at these different levels will reinforce and strengthen each other; having an impact

## Sample of Relevant Programs Funded by The California Endowment

| Program Name | What It Does |
| --- | --- |
| **Homeboy Industries Mental Health Education and Treatment Assistance Services** | Provides jobs and job training to at-risk youth and young adults in its small businesses in Los Angeles. Expanded its mental health and substance abuse counseling services and provided case management services to all participating in their job programs. |
| **San Diego Second Chance Reentry Advocacy Project** | Provides a set of comprehensive and integrated services that combines pre-release outreach with drug-. and alcohol-free housing, mental health counseling, and job training and placement after release to help released inmates adjust to reentry in San Diego. |
| **Youth UpRising PeaceMaking Program** | Provides—as part of Youth UpRising program—a set of cross-cutting, integrative services for at-risk youth in Oakland, including mentoring services and referrals to mental health resources, job training programs and educational opportunities. |
| **The Mentoring Center** | Provides a focused group-mentoring program known as Positive Minds Group On Location for youth most at risk of destructive behavior within three Bay Area schools. |
| **National League of Cities Institute's Gang Prevention Network** | Provides a coordinated effort that brings together civic and community leaders to develop and promote new approaches to reducing gang violence in 13 California cities—approaches that innovatively and comprehensively combine intervention, enforcement and prevention. |
| **Healthy Returns Initiative** | Provides improved access to health care for young offenders after release from the juvenile justice system in five California counties—Santa Clara, Santa Cruz, Ventura, Humboldt and Los Angeles— bringing together probation departments, health care providers, schools and families. |

on the odds for these young people is likely to require a portfolio of strategies. In sum, the unequal chances that boys and men of color face are not immutable, and we know an increasing amount about how to improve those chances.

The California Endowment has taken a leadership role in addressing the social determinants underlying such disparities that exist in California. This commissioned report is intended to contribute to the statewide conversation on this important set of issues by shedding light on key disparities within California for boys and men of color. This report is designed to help readers understand some of the basic facts related to the odds for boys and men of color in the state. But beyond that, we hope that the report will help identify starting points in the policy arena for diminishing the disparities for boys and men of color in California. The disparities in the indicators shown here can be used as a baseline to measure progress in narrowing inequalities over time.

# Acknowledgments

This work was sponsored by The California Endowment. We are particularly grateful for the guidance and feedback provided throughout the project by The California Endowment, including that from Alonzo Plough, Vice President, Strategy, Planning, and Evaluation; William Nicholas, Director of Research; and Robert Ross, President and Chief Executive Officer.

We owe a huge debt of gratitude for the insights provided by our technical reviewers—Gail Christopher, Vice President for Health of the W.K. Kellogg Foundation; Robert Valdez, Executive Director of the Robert Wood Johnson Foundation Center for Health Policy at the University of New Mexico; and John Engberg of RAND—as well as for overarching comments provided by Rebecca Collins of RAND Health.

Within RAND, we are grateful for the invaluable research assistance provided by Claire (Nailing) Xia, Sarah Outcault, Katie Mack, and Cali Ellis, as well as for the library assistance provided by Roberta Shanman and Ellen Kimmel. We also greatly benefited from administrative support provided by Lance Tan, support in preparing the document provided by Christopher Dirks, and support in overseeing the design, structure, and writing of the document and other communications products provided by Paul Steinberg.

Finally, while we appreciate the improvements provided by all those who have reviewed and commented on this document, we emphasize that the findings and recommendations, as well as any errors, are those of the authors alone.

# Abbreviations

| | |
|---|---|
| AIDS | Acquired Immune Deficiency Syndrome |
| BMI | Body Mass Index |
| CDC | Centers for Disease Control and Prevention |
| CDCR | California Department of Corrections and Rehabilitation |
| CHIS | California Health Interview Survey |
| CYA | California Youth Authority |
| DHS | California Department of Health Services |
| DHHS | Department of Health and Human Services |
| DJJ | Department of Juvenile Justice (California) |
| DVS | Developmental Victimization Survey |
| GAO | Government Accountability Office |
| HFNY | Healthy Families New York |
| HIV | Human Immunodeficiency Virus |
| ICD | International Classification of Diseases |
| IQ | Intelligence Quotient |
| NAEP | National Assessment of Educational Progress (U.S. Department of Education) |
| NFP | Nurse Family Partnership |
| OCR | Office of Civil Rights (U.S. Department of Education) |
| OHIR | Office of Health Information and Research (California Center for Health Statistics) |
| OJJDP | Office of Juvenile Justice and Delinquency Prevention (U.S. Department of Justice) |
| PPIC | Public Policy Institute of California |
| PPN | Promising Practices Network |
| PTSD | Post-Traumatic Stress Disorder |
| STD | Sexually Transmitted Disease |
| TAAG | Trial of Activity in Adolescent Girls |

"The *disparities* in the indicators shown here can be used as a baseline to *measure progress* in narrowing inequalities *over time*."

# Introduction

*An expanding body of literature has documented that racial and ethnic disparities exist across a broad array of domains (Williams and Collins, 1995; Krieger et al., 1993). The literature also addresses how racial and ethnic disparities have developed and persisted over time in the context of historical and structural racism that has shaped policies, practices and programs in ways that create disadvantage for certain groups (Aspen Institute Roundtable on Community Change, 2004; Hofrichter, 2003).*

This history and institutionalization of disadvantage has meant that "inequities that exist at all levels of society have persistent, profound, and long-lasting effects" (King County Equity and Social Justice Initiative, 2008). Within this context, boys and men of color are particularly vulnerable. The literature has found that inequities exist for boys and men of color across multiple domains. For example, boys and men of color have lower high school graduation rates, greater likelihood of going to prison, and higher mortality rates from homicide (Dellums Commission, 2006).

The California Endowment recently undertook a strategic planning process that focused on shifting its priorities toward community health and eliminating disparities. Given some alarming trends for people of color in areas such as high school completion rates and incarceration rates, The California Endowment recognizes what this means for the future of California communities of color. By elevating this area of work, its strategic plan now focuses on building and sustaining healthy communities. The California Endowment commissioned

"... boys and men of color have lower high school graduation rates, greater likelihood of going to prison and higher mortality rates from homicide."

this report to examine and document racial and ethnic disparities for boys and men of color in California. In recognition that many of these inequities are especially great for boys and men of color, The California Endowment asked us to focus specifically on this group as a starting point. A better understanding of the relative magnitude of the differences in life chances for boys and men of color in California will help to emphasize the significance of the problem, set the context for understanding how disparities manifest themselves over the life course, and identify what may be starting points for addressing these disparities. This report is designed to help readers better understand some of the basic facts related to the diminished life chances for boys and men of color in California.

We worked with The California Endowment to identify four broad domains—socioeconomic, health, safety, and ready to learn—and select specific individual-level indicators within each domain from a range of possibilities. We then analyzed the data to quantify the magnitude of the disparities.

- **Socioeconomic**. This domain relates to the socioeconomic conditions of boys and men of color as they develop. The indicators selected in this domain focus primarily on describing some of the individual-level characteristics of their social and economic environment.

- **Health**. This domain covers different aspects of the physical and emotional health of boys and men of color. The selected indicators focus on how they often start out life disadvantaged because of such circumstances as low birth weight, and how that disadvantage continues into childhood and adolescence with such health conditions as asthma and obesity.

- **Safety**. This domain encompasses both exposure to violence and contact with the criminal justice system for boys and men of color. The indicators in this domain include direct and indirect victimization, as well as arrest, incarceration and death rates.

- **Ready to Learn**. This domain focuses on how well boys and men of color are doing in school. The indicators selected in this domain include academic competence in different subject areas, high school completion and suspension.

While the indicators were examined independently within these outcome domains, together they contribute to overall well-being at an individual level. The indicators and domains are interrelated. In some cases, an indicator is a risk factor for one or more other indicators. And in other cases, poor outcomes on one indicator lead to poor outcomes on another indicator.

## A Standard Metric for Capturing Disparities

For each indicator in each outcome domain, we use a standard method for comparing the data and measuring the disparities. This method involves calculating the "odds" for boys and men of color—in this case, Latino and African-American boys and men—compared with white boys and men. What are the odds, for example, that an African-American or Latino boy will be arrested relative to a white boy, and how great is the disparity? By expressing the disparities in terms of odds, we provide a simple way to quantify the increased risk of one group over another.[3] If one group has higher odds than another, then that means there is a disparity between the groups for that indicator. For this report, we have calculated the odds by dividing the rate or percentage for boys and men of color by the rate or percentage for white boys and young men.

While any disproportion in odds is a concern, we focus on those indicators where the odds are *two times greater or more* for boys and men of color relative to their white peers. Specifically, we report on those indicators for which at least one of the groups (Latinos or African Americans) met the threshold of 2.0 higher odds than whites. Although this cut-off point is somewhat arbitrary, we believe that it serves as a useful starting point to help policymakers prioritize policy actions.

---

[3] We acknowledge that in the scientific community, the term "odds" has a more technical meaning that refers to the likelihood of an event occurring in one group. An "odds ratio" is then defined as the ratio of the odds of an event occurring in one group to the odds of it occurring in another group. In this report, we use the term odds more loosely to communicate the ratio of probabilities or rates.

Whenever possible, we provide male-only statistics, in keeping with the intent of The California Endowment. However, for some indicators, data by gender are simply not available. Likewise, we provide the odds for California only, unless only national data are available. In cases where such national data are available and where the differences provide a meaningful contrast, we compare California with the rest of the nation.

Before we move on to discuss what we found, it is important to note that in recent years surveys that collect data about racial and ethnic groups have modified how they categorize racial and ethnic identification. Some sources report data according to mutually exclusive categories, which distinguish between Hispanics who can be of any race and non-Hispanics of various racial groups. Some data are collected such that categories are not mutually exclusive, and data on Hispanic individuals are reported as well as data on all members of racial groups (Hispanic and non-Hispanic)[A]. To maintain consistency throughout the report, we use the term "African American" to refer to both black and non-Hispanic black data. We use the term "Latino" to refer to Hispanic data. The term "white" refers to both white and non-Hispanic white data. Finally, we did not include odds ratios for Asian children. This reflects the scarcity of available data for this group and the fact that the category of "Asian" captures a very diverse set of groups. There are likely to be different outcomes across subgroups—for example, between Chinese, Japanese, Vietnamese and Cambodian children—all of which are part of the broad Asian category. Subgroup analysis was beyond the scope of the current study.

## What Lies Ahead

In Chapter Two, we provide readers with some context for how we examined the diminished life chances of boys and men of color and describe the conceptual framework that grounds our coverage of this issue. This chapter also provides readers with a brief sketch of the demographics of California.

[A] As a result, in some data instances, Hispanics or Latinos are included in the counts for racial groups. Thus, rate comparisons between whites and Latinos can result in the "white rates" being underestimates making the relative differences between the rates for whites and Latinos less than what they truly are and thus, the "odds" will appear smaller or lower. When available, we report data according to mutually exclusive categories and we note in Chapter 3 where this occurs.

In Chapter Three, which forms the core of the report, we examine the odds for the selected indicators in each of the four outcome areas, providing details on the odds and showing the disparities we find graphically. What emerges from the chapter is a wealth of detailed data across indicators and outcomes. It tells us where boys and men of color now stand relative to their white counterparts.

The data presented in Chapter Three tell us where disparities for boys and men of color exist among the selected indicators. Chapter Four reviews some strategies for reducing the disparities for boys and young men of color, including effective programs, practices and policies.

Finally, Chapter Five summarizes the significance of this report and some of the main findings.

"*While any disproportion in odds is a concern, we focus on those indicators where the odds are two times greater or more for boys and men of color relative to their white peers.*"

# Disparities in a Social Determinant Context

*Before launching into the core of the report, we provide some context to help make sense of what our analysis of the odds of boys and men and color relative to their white counterparts means. Here, we present the conceptual framework that underpins that analysis, as well as a brief overview of the demographics of California.*

## Grounding our Analysis – A Conceptual Framework

While the focus of this report is individual-level outcomes, these outcomes are the manifestation of a spectrum of environmental, social, family and individual factors that operate together to influence individual development. In trying to understand where disparities come from and how to address them, we grounded our research in the context of a conceptual framework based on the Northridge, Sclar, and Biswas (2003) model which describes the contextual factors that interact to promote or inhibit individual health outcomes. This model highlights the multiple pathways by which factors in the physical, social, economic, and family domains contribute to individual well-being. We modified their framework to include safety and education (or ready to learn) outcomes at the individual level (see **Table 2.1**).

At the macro level, social factors, such as cultural institutions, economic and political systems and ideologies interact with inequalities in wealth, employment and educational opportunities and political influence. These inequalities, in turn, also influence the social context in which a child develops. These fundamental underlying macro-level factors, such as the historical context and the cultural and natural environment, may be particularly challenging to overcome at a policy level. Together, the macro-level forces influence communities through the built environment and social context.

*"… social factors interact with inequalities… These inequalities, in turn, also influence the social context in which a child develops.*

At the community level, the built environment includes such factors as land use, availability of services and transportation, recreational resources (such as parks), and the type of housing and schools available. A community's social context takes into account the quality of education, local policies, political influence, and the amount of community investment. As noted by Northridge, Sclar, and Biswas (2003), the built environment and social context also represent where policy interventions such as land-use policies or economic development have an important potential to influence health and other outcomes at the population and individual levels.

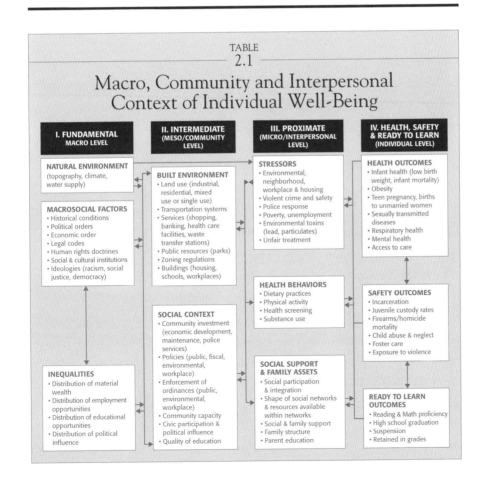

TABLE
2.1

## Macro, Community and Interpersonal Context of Individual Well-Being

| I. FUNDAMENTAL MACRO LEVEL | II. INTERMEDIATE (MESO/COMMUNITY LEVEL) | III. PROXIMATE (MICRO/INTERPERSONAL LEVEL) | IV. HEALTH, SAFETY & READY TO LEARN (INDIVIDUAL LEVEL) |
|---|---|---|---|
| **NATURAL ENVIRONMENT** (topography, climate, water supply) | **BUILT ENVIRONMENT** • Land use (industrial, residential, mixed use or single use) • Transportation systems • Services (shopping, banking, health care facilities, waste transfer stations) • Public resources (parks) • Zoning regulations • Buildings (housing, schools, workplaces) | **STRESSORS** • Environmental, neighborhood, workplace & housing • Violent crime and safety • Police response • Poverty, unemployment • Environmental toxins (lead, particulates) • Unfair treatment | **HEALTH OUTCOMES** • Infant health (low birth weight, infant mortality) • Obesity • Teen pregnancy, births to unmarried women • Sexually transmitted diseases • Respiratory health • Mental health • Access to care |
| **MACROSOCIAL FACTORS** • Historical conditions • Political orders • Economic order • Legal codes • Human rights doctrines • Social & cultural institutions • Ideologies (racism, social justice, democracy) | | **HEALTH BEHAVIORS** • Dietary practices • Physical activity • Health screening • Substance use | **SAFETY OUTCOMES** • Incarceration • Juvenile custody rates • Firearms/homicide mortality • Child abuse & neglect • Foster care • Exposure to violence |
| **INEQUALITIES** • Distribution of material wealth • Distribution of employment opportunities • Distribution of educational opportunities • Distribution of political influence | **SOCIAL CONTEXT** • Community investment (economic development, maintenance, police services) • Policies (public, fiscal, environmental, workplace) • Enforcement of ordinances (public, environmental, workplace) • Community capacity • Civic participation & political influence • Quality of education | **SOCIAL SUPPORT & FAMILY ASSETS** • Social participation & integration • Shape of social networks & resources available within networks • Social & family support • Family structure • Parent education | **READY TO LEARN OUTCOMES** • Reading & Math proficiency • High school graduation • Suspension • Retained in grades |

## FIGURE 2.1

### Percent distribution by age and by race and Hispanic origin, California and the U.S., 2006.

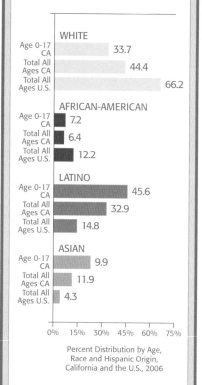

**WHITE**
- Age 0-17 CA: 33.7
- Total All Ages CA: 44.4
- Total All Ages U.S.: 66.2

**AFRICAN-AMERICAN**
- Age 0-17 CA: 7.2
- Total All Ages CA: 6.4
- Total All Ages U.S.: 12.2

**LATINO**
- Age 0-17 CA: 45.6
- Total All Ages CA: 32.9
- Total All Ages U.S.: 14.8

**ASIAN**
- Age 0-17 CA: 9.9
- Total All Ages CA: 11.9
- Total All Ages U.S.: 4.3

0%  15%  30%  45%  60%  75%

Percent Distribution by Age, Race and Hispanic Origin, California and the U.S., 2006

*Sources: United States: U.S. Census Bureau, 2006, and U.S. Census Bureau, 2008. California: California Department of Finance, 2007a. Note: Percentages may not sum to 100 because of rounding and exclusion of other races.*

At the micro/interpersonal level, stressors can include such factors as violent crime, unsafe housing, financial insecurity or unfair treatment. In terms of social support and family assets, neighborhood social cohesion, family, social support, and parent education are also important contributors to an individual's development and well-being. In addition, individual health behaviors, including substance use, dietary practices and physical activity are also important influences on outcomes. Together, these micro-level factors impact the individual-level outcomes in the final column of **Table 2.1**.

Three key aspects of this framework are important in considering the results we present. First, individual outcomes and behavior are not generated in isolation, but rather are embedded in a social and economic context. Second, the individual-level outcomes are likely to be related, because they are produced in the same underlying context. Third, this framework captures the complex set of factors that contribute to disparities in the odds for boys and young men of color, as discussed in the vast literature on this subject (see, for example, Hofrichter, 2003; Western, 2006; Dellums Commission, 2006). We return to this framework again in Chapter Four, when we discuss approaches to diminishing the disparities for boys and young men of color.

## Overview of California Demographics

In understanding the impact of whatever disparities exist for boys and men of color in California, it is critical to know a little about the state's demographics. In 2006, 12.5 percent of the U.S. population lived in California (California Department of Finance, 2007a), making California first in the ranking of states according to population. However, California demographics do not match those of the rest of the nation: Californians are less likely to be white or black and are more likely to be foreign-born. According to data from 2006, Californians were about two and a quarter times more likely to be Latino than other U.S. residents and nearly three times more likely to be Asian (as shown in **Figure 2.1**). In contrast, Californians were about half as likely as the U.S. population to be black and less than two-thirds as likely to be white. As of 2005, over a quarter (27.2 percent) of Californians were foreign-born compared with 12.4 percent of the U.S. population (U.S. Census Bureau, 2008, Table 40).

While less than a third of all Californians were Latino in the 2000 Census, close to half of children in California age 0–5 were Latino (California Department of Finance, 2007a). Across the age distribution, younger Californians are more likely to be Latino and are less likely to come from other racial and ethnic groups. It is clear that future generations of boys and men of color in California are going to be predominantly Latino. In fact, boys and men of color between the ages of 15 and 20 in 2015 will be 1.3 times more likely to be Asian than African-American, about 7.5 times more likely to be Latino than African-American, and about two-thirds more likely to be multiracial than African-American.

This overview highlights the large number of Asian boys and men in California compared with the rest of the nation. However, our review of the data and research does not reflect the numerical *heft* of this group: Data on Asian youth are less often available than data for whites, African Americans, and Latinos. Another important caveat to the generalizations we present here for Asians is that this group includes an extremely diverse set of ethnic and cultural groups, ranging from Southeast Asian immigrants from Cambodia, Vietnam, and Laos—groups who experience some of the greatest disadvantages of any groups of youth—to Asian youth who come from some of the wealthiest industrialized nations in the world, such as Japan.

# Addressing Disparities Faced by Boys and Men of Color in California

*Now we present data for the indicators of well-being where boys and men of color in California fare worse than their white peers. This chapter is intended to help policymakers identify the areas where boys and men of color could gain the most ground.*

We wanted to select indicators that met several important standards for indicators of children's well-being (Moore, 1997). This meant several things. First, we wanted the indicators to be comprehensive—that is, we wanted them to represent well-being across a range of outcomes and behaviors. Second, we wanted them to be cogent, so that readers would find them relevant and understandable. Third, we wanted to be able to track the indicators in the future, so we wanted to include indicators where the data were readily available to allow analysts, community planners and policymakers to assess progress over time.

Given our desire for indicators that meet these standards, we started by selecting a set of potential indicators for consideration. We began by reviewing numerous well-known national indicator projects to obtain a comprehensive set of indicators used in other efforts. These included KIDS COUNT (Annie E. Casey Foundation, 2007), the Federal Interagency Forum on Child and Family Statistics key indicators report (2007), Los Angeles Children's Planning Council scorecards (2006), Hauser, Brown, and Prosser (1997), and others. We then conferred with The California Endowment about their areas of strategic interests. This harvesting of potential indicators netted more than a hundred indicators.

"*While poverty rates are extremely high among families without a working parent (73 percent), most poor children have a working parent…*"

Reflecting the framework shown in Chapter Two, we organized the indicators into four outcome domains: socioeconomic, health, safety, and ready to learn. Working with The California Endowment, we then narrowed the list by selecting indicators within each domain that have been frequently used in other national indicator projects. We considered this a proxy for their being an important social goal. We also focused on indicators that met the standards mentioned above. Finally, since we wanted to present data for boys and men of color in California, we focused on indicators where we expected to be able to obtain reliable data by gender, race or Hispanic origin.

This process netted a total of 61 indicators in the four domains. For each indicator, we calculated the "odds" for boys and men of color—in this case, African-American and Latino boys and men—compared with white boys and men. We determined the odds by dividing the rate or percentage for African-American or Latino boys and men by the rate or percentage for white boys or men. For example, the infant mortality rate for African-American male infants is 13.5 per 1,000 births. The corresponding rate for white male infants is 4.9 per 1,000. The odds are then calculated by dividing 13.5 by 4.9. In this example, the infant mortality rate for African-American male infants is 2.8 times greater than the rate for white male infants.[4]

Whenever possible, we present these odds for California only. If data are only available at the national level, then we present the national figures. Likewise, whenever possible, we present data only for boys and men; however, some data are not available by gender. For those indicators, we present the data for both males and females.

Rather than presenting data for all the indicators examined in the body of this report, we present here information for those indicators where the odds are *two times or more* for boys and men of color relative to whites, and those that are most commonly used to characterize the four domains. Each subsection

---

[4] Note that there is technical meaning for an "odds ratio" used by demographers and other social scientists. This is calculated by dividing the likelihood of an event occurring in one group by the likelihood of the event occurring in another group.

below presents the findings for those indicators; in the appendix we provide the detailed results for the indicators with odds lower than 2.0 and for the indicators that are similar to some of those in the main report. (For example, we present only one indicator for sexually-transmitted diseases in the main report and others in the appendix.) It could reasonably be argued that any disparity in odds is undesirable, or that instead of disparities, absolute levels relative to some socially desirable level is a good standard. Readers who are interested in making these types of comparisons can use the findings in this document along with the data in the appendix.

## Socioeconomic Disparities

In the socioeconomic outcome area, we considered indicators related to families' economic well-being, household structure and parental education. For four of the indicators we examined—shown in **Table 3.1**—the odds for boys and young men of color were two times higher or more than they are for white counterparts. We present data on these indicators below.

### Children Living in Poverty

California has experienced higher child poverty rates than the country as a whole since the early 1980s. Between 2002 and 2005, the child poverty rate remained about 19 percent overall. African-American and Latino children in

TABLE
3.1

## Socioeconomic Outcome Indicators with Odds for Boys and Men of Color Greater Than Twice What They Are for White Boys and Men

| Children living in poverty | Single-parent household |
| --- | --- |
| Maternal education (less than high school) | Unemployed parent |

California experience the highest rates of child poverty—each at about 27 percent (as shown in **Figure 3.1**). The figure compares African-American and Latino children relative to white children and shows the disparities in percentage terms—8 percent versus 27 percent. The odds ratios, calculated by dividing 27 by 8 are 3.4, shown inside the bars. Slightly more than half of the children in poverty in California are Latino.

California poverty rates are associated with family structure, parental education and parental work status. Families with a single mother have the highest poverty rates, at 42 percent, while married-couple families have a rate of only 12 percent. About half of the poor children in California live in families in which neither parent finished high school; the rate of poverty in these families is 44 percent. While poverty rates are extremely high among families without a working parent (73 percent), most poor children have a working parent: 34 percent have a parent who works full-time, and 39 percent have a parent who works part-time (Public Policy Institute of California, 2006).

### Maternal Education (Less Than High School)

**Figure 3.2** shows that white and African-American mothers in California tend to be more educated than their counterparts in the rest of the United States, but that this advantage is not as great for Latino mothers. African-American mothers are about two times more likely than white mothers of children in this age group to have less than a high school education in 2005, and Latino mothers are more than ten times more likely than white mothers to have less than a high school education (see **Figure 3.2**).

Several decades of research have demonstrated strong links between maternal education and a range of child outcomes (for example, Coleman et al., 1966; Leibowitz, 1977; McLanahan, 2004; and Carneiro, Meghir, and Parey, 2007). Such research has argued that maternal education may improve children's well-being, both because maternal education is highly correlated with other

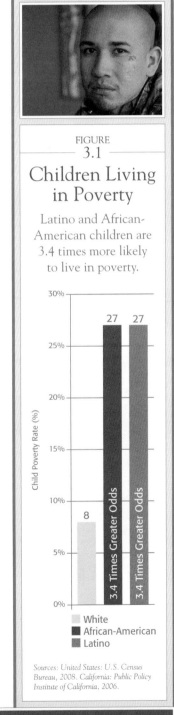

FIGURE
3.1

# Children Living in Poverty

Latino and African-American children are 3.4 times more likely to live in poverty.

Sources: United States: U.S. Census Bureau, 2008. California: Public Policy Institute of California, 2006.

## Mothers With No High School Degree

Latino mothers are 10.2 times more likely to have less than a high school degree; African-American mothers are 2.0 times as likely to have less than a high school degree.

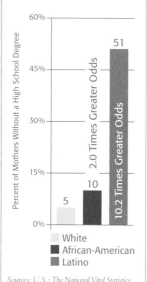

Sources: U.S.: The National Vital Statistics System (National Center for Health Statistics, 2007a). California: Authors' calculations from the 2005 California Health Interview Survey (California Health Interview Survey, 2007a and 2007b).

socioeconomic determinants of children's outcomes—such as family income and neighborhood quality—and also because maternal education is associated with better caregiving, resulting in better health practices, home literacy, and other behaviors that promote child development (Desai and Alva, 1998).

### Children in Single-Parent Households

Children and youth in single-parent families fare worse on a range of outcomes compared with children in two-parent families (Painter and Levine, 2000). In California in 2005, nearly a quarter (24.4 percent) of female-headed single-parent families lived in poverty and 10 percent of male-headed single-parent families lived in poverty. The rate for families headed by a couple was 7.2 percent, and 77.3 percent of families in poverty reported that they had children (California Department of Finance, 2007). As shown in **Figure 3.3**, among families with children, African-American families in California are two and a half times more likely to be headed by one parent than white families. The rate of Latino single-parent families with children is only slightly higher than that of whites (1.1 times).

There are a number of reasons that household structure is important for child development. Having one parent instead of two generally implies that there are fewer monetary, time, and other resources to devote to child rearing (Kilburn and Wolfe, 2002). Furthermore, single-parent families typically have less social capital, given their smaller social networks, and they tend to live in less enriching neighborhoods. Children who experience a divorce also may have to contend with the stress of being separated from a parent, potential moves and school changes, and possible parental disagreements and remarriages (Painter and Levine, 2000). Hence, household structure may have implications for child development independent of the effects from resource availability.

### Children with Unemployed Parents

As mentioned above, parents' work status is highly associated with child poverty. In California in 2005, the median family income was $60,000. For families with no employed adult, the median family income was $25,649 (California Department of Finance, 2007). Recent data on parental employment by race and Latino origin were not available for California, but we identified recent national data on parental full-time, full-year employment (Federal Interagency Forum on Child and Family Statistics, 2007). As shown in **Figure 3.4**, these data show that 16 percent of white families have no parent employed year-round full-time, compared with 38 percent of African-American families and 26 percent of Latino families. The odds of parental unemployment are 2.4 times greater for African-American families and 1.6 times greater for Latino families than for white families.

## Health Disparities

Health disparities cover a range of physical health and social and emotional well-being outcomes, as well as access to health care and insurance. We have organized this section to look across the life course, beginning with a child's birth and moving up through early adulthood, in summarizing the disproportionate odds for boys and men of color.

**Table 3.2** shows a list of the health indicators where we find that the odds for boys and men of color were two times higher or more than their white counterparts. In the remainder of this section, we focus on discussing these indicators.

### Low Birth Weight

A child's developmental path begins at birth. Very low birth weight is the percentage of infants born at less than 1,500 grams (3 pounds, 4 ounces). Low birth weight is defined as the percentage of infants born between 1,500

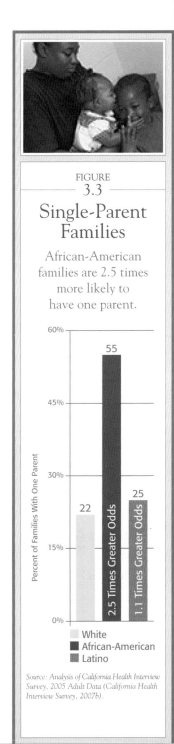

FIGURE
3.3

# Single-Parent Families

African-American families are 2.5 times more likely to have one parent.

Source: Analysis of California Health Interview Survey, 2005 Adult Data (California Health Interview Survey, 2007b).

and 2,500 grams (5 pounds, 8 ounces). African-American infants begin their development at a disadvantage relative to white infants. In California, the odds of a very low birth weight birth are 2.6 times greater for African-American infants than for white infants or Latino infants (see **Figure 3.5**). The odds for low birth weight are 1.9 times higher for African-American infants. Nationally, 8.2 percent of infants were born at low birth weight in 2005. There are notable differences depending on race and ethnicity. African-American infants (14 percent) are about twice as likely to be low birth weight as white (7.3 percent) and Latino infants (6.9 percent).

While Latinos and African Americans both fare poorly on many socioeconomic factors, the data indicate that Latino children do not suffer the same negative outcomes as African-American children. Here, we see that Latino children are not at increased risk for low birth weight. This phenomenon where Latinos exhibit better than expected outcomes despite poor socioeconomic conditions is often referred to as the "Hispanic Paradox" (Franzini, Ribble, and Keddie,

FIGURE
3.4

## Unemployed Parents

African-American families are 2.4 times more likely to not have parents employed year-round, full-time.

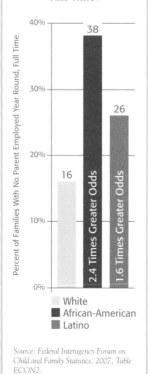

White
African-American
Latino

Source: Federal Interagency Forum on Child and Family Statistics, 2007, Table ECON2.

TABLE
3.2

## Health Outcome Indicators with Odds for Boys and Men of Color Greater Than Twice What They Are for White Boys and Men

| | |
|---|---|
| Low birth weight | Childhood obesity |
| Births to unmarried women | Post-Traumatic Stress Disorder (PTSD) |
| Births to teen mothers | Health insurance (lack of) |
| Infant mortality | Access to health care (no usual source of care) |
| Childhood asthma-related hospitalizations | HIV and AIDS |

2001). Some of the reasons for the variation in low and very low birth weight across race and ethnicity include socioeconomic status, maternal education, insurance status parental birth weight status, and length of gestation (Nanyonio et al., Conley and Bennett, 2000). Some research has shown that neighborhood unemployment and low birth weight are related, with higher neighborhood unemployment rates correlated with lower birth weight among African-American infants (Pearl, Braveman, and Abrams, 2001).

When a child is born with low birth weight, he starts the developmental process at risk for a variety of poor outcomes. Low birth weight is related to poor morbidity and mortality. Low birth weight infants are also more likely to have poor neurological, cognitive, behavioral and academic outcomes than infants born at a normal weight. An infant with low birth weight is also at increased risk for neurological conditions such as cerebral palsy, lower scores on IQ tests, behavioral problems such as conduct disorder and hyperactivity, and illnesses such as asthma, respiratory infections and ear infections (Hack, Klein, and Taylor, 1995). Low birth weight infants also have higher mortality risk than infants born at a normal weight. Mortality for low birth weight infants is about eight times higher than for normal weight infants (Mathews, Menacker, and MacDorman, 2002). Some of the risk factors for low birth weight include maternal smoking, infections, inadequate prenatal care, low maternal weight gain, maternal or fetal stress and pregnancy complications (Ricketts, Murray, and Schwalberg, 2005).

### Births to Unmarried Women

In California, the percentage of births to unmarried women is three times greater for African-American infants and 2.2 times greater for Latino infants when compared with white infants (as shown in **Figure 3.6**). Nationally, about 39 percent of all births nationwide are to unmarried women, with notable differences depending on race or ethnicity. The percentage of births to unmarried women was 2.7 times greater for non-Hispanic

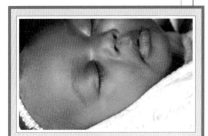

FIGURE
3.5

## Low Birth Weight Infants

African-American infants are 2.6 times more likely to be *very low* birth weight and 1.9 times more likely to be *low* birth weight.

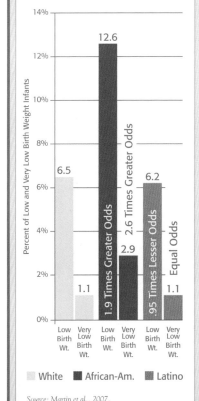

Source: Martin et al., 2007.

African-American women when compared with non-Hispanic white women. For Hispanic women, the percentage of births to unmarried women was 1.9 times greater than that of non-Hispanic white women (Martin et al., 2007).

The odds of poor outcomes also increase when a child is born to an unmarried woman. Children who are born out of wedlock are at increased risk for a variety of negative outcomes across their lifespan. Early on, a child born to an unmarried woman is more likely to live in poverty and have an unstable home environment. There is also evidence that children born to unmarried women experience more symptoms of depression. During adolescence, children born to unmarried women are at increased risk of dropping out of school, having sexual intercourse or becoming parents. As young adults, those born to an unmarried woman arc also more likely to be unemployed and have marital problems (Amato, 2005; Aquilino, 1996).

### Births to Teen Mothers

In California, the odds of an infant being born to a teenage mother are 3.6 times greater for Latino infants than for white infants (see **Figure 3.7**). African-American infants are more than twice as likely as white infants to be born to a teenage mother. Nationally, the birth rate for females ages 15 to 19 was about 42 per 1,000 in 2006. The rate varied by the teenager's race or ethnicity. The odds of becoming a teenage mother were 3.1 times higher for Hispanic girls compared with non-Hispanic white girls. Non-Hispanic African-American girls were 2.4 times more likely than non-Hispanic white girls to become teenage mothers (Hamilton, Martin, and Ventura, 2007).

Children that are born to teenage mothers are at increased risk for a variety of poor health, education and safety outcomes. In terms of their health, the children of teenage mothers are more likely to be low birth weight and less likely to receive medical care, despite greater health needs. Children that are born to teenage mothers also have decreased odds of success in school and

FIGURE
3.6

## Births to Unmarried Women

African-American infants are 3 times more likely to be born to an unmarried woman; Latino infants are 2.2 times more likely.

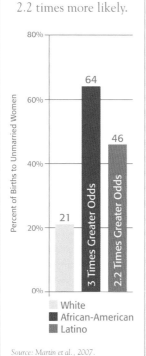

Source: Martin et al., 2007.

future employment. When a child is born to a teenage mother, he has a greater chance of repeating a grade, dropping out of high school or being unemployed as a young adult. Children of teenage mothers are also not as safe. They are more likely to be the victims of child abuse and neglect, to run away from home, and to end up in prison later in life (Maynard, 1997).

Many of the risk factors for teenage pregnancy are related to the child's socioeconomic status. Poverty, low education level, and lack of employment are all predictors of teenage pregnancy for teenagers of all racial and ethnic groups (Kirby, Coyle, and Gould, 2001). For Latinos, high teenage pregnancy rates are also related to cultural attitudes and norms about parental communication, marriage, family formation and early motherhood (Russell et al., 2004).

### Infant Mortality

Despite improvements in the health of African Americans, African-American infants are still much more likely than white babies to die before their first birthday (Saenz, 2007). In California, African-American male infants have nearly three times the infant mortality rate of white male infants, while Latino male infants are about 1.2 times more likely to die than white infants (see **Figure 3.8**).

Although the infant mortality rate has declined for both African Americans and whites over the past three decades, the disparity between these two social groups persists (Wise, 2003). While infant mortality rates declined during the late 1980s and 1990s for all racial and ethnic groups, the 20 percent decline for African Americans was somewhat slower than that for other groups (Kung et al., 2007). Since 2000, the infant mortality rate has remained relatively stable. Infant mortality is associated with a number of factors, including low birth weight, socioeconomic status, a mother's age, nutrition, maternal education and lack of prenatal care (Kung et al., 2007).

FIGURE
—— 3.7 ——

## Births to Teen Mothers

Latino infants are 3.6 times more likely to be born to teenage mothers; African-American infants are 2.2 times more likely.

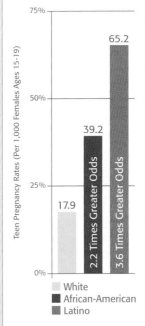

Source: Kidsdata.org, "Teen Births: Teen Birth Rate, by Race/Ethnicity: 2003," Web page, 2008.

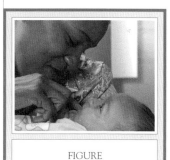

FIGURE
3.8

## Infant Mortality

African-American male infants are 2.8 times more likely to die before their first birthday.

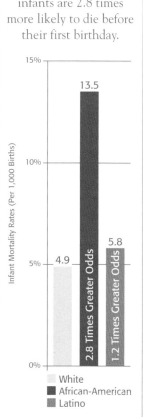

Infant Mortality Rates (Per 1,000 Births)

15%

13.5

10%

5%

4.9

5.8

2.8 Times Greater Odds

1.2 Times Greater Odds

0%

White
African-American
Latino

*Source: California Department of Health Care Services, 2007c.*

## Childhood Asthma

In California, the odds of having active asthma are 1.7 times higher for African-American children than they are for white children; in addition, 7 percent of Latino children have active asthma (Meng et al., 2007). Nationally, 9 percent of children 18 years of age or younger have active asthma, compared with 8.6 percent of children under age 18 in California (Bloom and Cohen, 2007; California Department of Health Services, 2007). Active asthma is defined as those individuals who have been diagnosed with asthma and who reported they still had asthma and/or experienced an asthma attack in the past year. Disproportionality in asthma burden among California children can be measured by differences in hospitalization rates. African-American male children had asthma hospitalization rates 3.7 times greater than their white counterparts (see **Figure 3.9**).

Asthma is a common chronic inflammatory disorder of the airways among children. Asthma morbidity and mortality are largely preventable with adequate medication, management and patient education. Risk factors for asthma include living in an urban area (especially the inner city, which may increase exposure to environmental pollutants) substandard housing, respiratory infections in childhood, low birth weight, obesity, having one or both parents with asthma or exposure to secondhand smoke (Mayo Clinic, 2008; California Department of Health Services, 2007). In children, asthma is an important reason for missed school days, and asthma exacerbations can result in emergency department visits and hospitalizations (Moorman et al., 2007).

## Childhood Obesity

In California, obesity among children and adolescents is a serious public health problem. Among adolescents ages 12 to 17, Latinos are twice as likely to be overweight (see **Figure 3.10**). Overweight or obese is defined as having a body mass index (BMI) in the 95th percentile with respect to weight and gender.

Obesity rates are rising faster in African-American and Latino populations than among whites, with the rise in obesity rates foreshadowing even greater disparities in diabetes, cardiovascular disease and other chronic diseases. (Dubowitz et al., forthcoming). Nationally, the prevalence of obesity is significantly higher in Latino boys than in African-American and white boys (National Center for Health Statistics, 2007). Obesity is related to lifestyle, environment and genes, with a number of underlying factors including neighborhood characteristics (e.g., neighborhood socioeconomic status, high crime).

### Post-Traumatic Stress Disorder

Post-traumatic stress disorder (PTSD) has been found to disproportionately affect boys and young men of color. Nationally, the odds of an African-American adolescent having PTSD are 2.5 times greater than that of a white adolescent (see **Figure 3.11**). Compared with white adolescents, Latino adolescents have 4.1 times greater odds of having PTSD (Kilpatrick et al., 2003). Nationally, the overall six-month PTSD prevalence rate for adolescent boys is 3.7 percent. These data come from a national probability sample of adolescents 12 to 17 years of age and represent the results of hierarchical logistic regression

FIGURE
3.9

## Children's Hospitalization for Asthma

African-American boys and adolescents are 3.7 times more likely to be hospitalized for asthma.

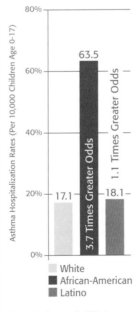

Asthma Hospitalization Rates (Per 10,000 Children Age 0-17)

80%

60% — 63.5

40%

20% — 17.1    18.1

0%

17.1 — 3.7 Times Greater Odds
18.1 — 1.1 Times Greater Odds

■ White
■ African-American
■ Latino

*Source: Stockman et al., 2004. Age adjusted to the 2000 U.S. population.*

FIGURE
3.10

## Childhood Obesity

Latino boys are twice as likely to be overweight.

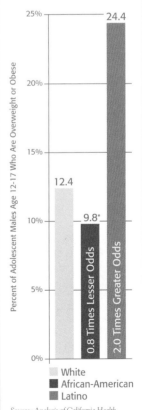

Percent of Adolescent Males Age 12-17 Who Are Overweight or Obese

25% — 24.4

20%

15%

12.4

10% — 9.8*

5%

0%

9.8* — 0.8 Times Lesser Odds
24.4 — 2.0 Times Greater Odds

■ White
■ African-American
■ Latino

*Source: Analysis of California Health Interview Survey, 2005 Adolescent Data, California Health Interview Survey, 2007a).
*Estimate for African-American males is statistically unreliable due to small cell size.*

FIGURE
3.11

## Adolescent Post-Traumatic Stress Disorder

African-American adolescents are 2.5 times more likely to exhibit symptoms of PTSD; Latino adolescents are 4.1 times as likely.

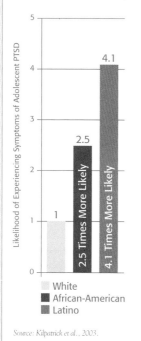

White
African-American
Latino

*Source: Kilpatrick et al., 2003.*

models to examine the relationship of age, gender and race and ethnicity to the risk of PTSD.

PTSD emerges after traumatic events that threaten serious harm to an individual, both physically and emotionally. For children and adolescents, the types of traumatic events that may lead to PTSD include natural disasters, exposure to interpersonal violence, accidents, war and violent crime. Studies have shown that direct victimization and multiple exposures increase the likelihood of developing PTSD. For children who have been exposed to a traumatic event, the severity of the event, the parental reaction to it, and the physical proximity to the event all influence the development of PTSD. The symptoms of PTSD include reliving the event, psychological numbing or avoidance behavior and increased irritability. PTSD in adolescents often manifests itself as increased impulsive and aggressive behavior. Adolescents with PTSD are more likely to perform poorly at school and to become juvenile delinquents (Cohen, 1998).

### Health Insurance

Nationally, 89 percent of children had health insurance coverage in 2005 at some point during the year. But that left approximately 8.1 million children (11 percent) with no insurance at any time during 2005. Latino children are less likely than white, non-Hispanic or African-American children to have health insurance (Federal Interagency Forum on Child and Family Statistics, 2007). In California, Latino boys and adolescents ages birth to 17 are 4.8 times as likely as white boys and adolescents to be currently uninsured (see **Figure 3.12**).

Many of California's children are covered by public insurance programs. Between 2001 and 2005, employer-based coverage for children declined by 5 percentage points (Brown et al., 2007). During this same time period, the percentage of children enrolled continuously in Medi-Cal or Healthy Families increased from 24 percent to 31 percent (Brown et al., 2007).

Among uninsured children who were eligible for public insurance, Latino children were the least likely to be enrolled.

### Access to Health Care

Whether children and adolescents have a usual source of medical care is one important measure of access to health care. In California, Latino boys are 2.5 more times as likely than white boys to not have a usual source of medical care (see **Figure 3.13**). Nationally, 10.9 percent of Latino children did not have a usual source of medical care in 2006, compared with 5.1 percent of white children and 4.1 percent of African-American children (Bloom and Cohen, 2007).

### HIV and AIDS

Nationally, the risk of contracting HIV or AIDS[5] is 6.9 times higher for African-American male adults and adolescents than for whites. Latinos are 3.1 times more likely than whites to have HIV or AIDS (see **Figure 3.14**). HIV works against the immune system and allows infections to grow and spread throughout the body; it is most commonly transmitted through sexual contact and injection drug use.

In California, HIV-related mortality is the eighth leading cause of death for African-American men and the tenth leading cause for Latino

[5] The data includes persons with a diagnosis of HIV infection (not AIDS), a diagnosis of HIV infection and a later diagnosis of AIDS, or concurrent diagnoses of HIV infection and AIDS.

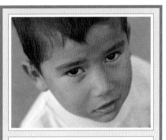

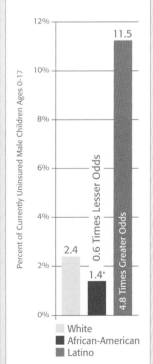

FIGURE
3.12

# Uninsured Children

Latino boys and adolescents are 4.8 times more likely to be uninsured.

Source: Analysis of California Health Interview Survey, 2005 adolescent data (California Health Interview Survey, 2007a). "Currently uninsured" means those children uninsured at the time of the CHIS interview. *Estimate for African-American males is statistically unreliable due to small cell size.

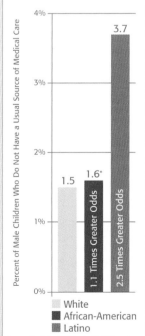

FIGURE
3.13

# Children Without a Usual Source of Medical Care
(0 – 11 Years)

Latino boys are 2.5 times as likely to be without a usual source of medical care than white boys.

Source: Analysis of California Health Interview Survey, 2005 adolescent data (California Health Interview Survey, 2007a). *Estimate for African-American boys is statistically reliable due to small cell size.

FIGURE
——— 3.14 ———
# HIV and AIDS

African-American male
adults and adolescents are
6.9 times more likely to
have HIV or AIDS; Latinos
are 3.1 times more likely.

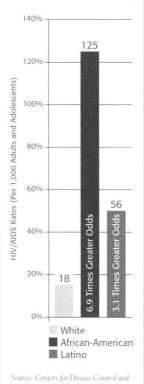

Figure bars: White 18, African-American 125 (6.9 Times Greater Odds), Latino 56 (3.1 Times Greater Odds). Y-axis: HIV/AIDS Rates (Per 1,000 Adults and Adolescents).

Legend: White, African-American, Latino

*Source: Centers for Disease Control and Prevention, 2007.*

men.[6] African-American men have a mortality rate from HIV infection nearly four times higher than that of white and Latino men (Lee and McConville, 2007).[7]

## Safety

The safety outcome domain encompasses two broad categories—exposure to violence and contact with the juvenile justice and adult criminal justice systems. We have organized this section beginning with the indicators related to victimization and exposure to violence and then moving on to those related to criminal justice system involvement. **Table 3.3** provides a list of the indicators examined in the safety domain where we find the odds for boys and men of color were two times or more than their white counterparts. In the remainder of this section, we focus on discussing these indicators.

TABLE
——— 3.3 ———
### Safety Outcome Indicators with Odds for Boys and Men of Color Greater Than Twice What They Are for White Boys and Men

| | |
|---|---|
| Witnessing domestic violence | Disproportional representation in prison population |
| Exposure to other forms of violence | Incarceration rate |
| Substantiated child abuse and neglect | Children with incarcerated parents |
| Foster care | Firearms-related death rate |
| Juvenile arrest and custody rates | Homicide-related death rate |
| Lifetime likelihood of ever going to prison | |

[6] In comparison, HIV-related mortality is the 13th leading cause of death for white men and 21st leading cause for Asian men in California.
[7] For adult African-American men, there were 47.2 HIV-related deaths per 100,000 compared with 10.9 HIV-related deaths per 100,000 for white men and 11.6 HIV-related deaths per 100,000 for Latino men. California Department of Health Services (DHS) death certificate data (2000-2002) and the 2000 decennial census were used to calculate leading causes of death. The cause-of-death coding is based on the International Classification of Diseases, tenth revision (ICD-10).

## Witnessing Domestic Violence and Exposure to Other Forms of Violence

The Developmental Victimization Survey (DVS), conducted in 2002 and 2003, was designed to fill an information void related to children's exposure to violence (Finkelhor et al., 2005).[8] Nationally, African-American children and youth have significantly higher odds of witnessing domestic violence or being exposed to shootings, bombs or riots when compared with white children and youth (see **Figure 3.15**). The odds of an African-American child witnessing domestic violence are more than twice that of a white child. African-American children and youth are nearly 3 times as likely to witness a shooting, bombing or riot. Similarly, Latino children and youth are just over 2 times more likely to witness a shooting, bombing or riot than white children and youth.

In addition, the odds of an African-American child or youth of having someone close to them murdered is 7.8 times more than a white child or youth; a Latino child's odds are 7.4 times more than a white child or youth (Finkelhor et al., 2005).

A child's exposure to violence can have consequences for his development. Children exposed to violence are more likely to have internalizing and externalizing behavior problems (Peled, Jaffe, and Edleson, 1995). Children who witness violence are at increased risk for becoming victims themselves, suffering from PTSD, abusing alcohol or drugs, running away from home or engaging in criminal activity (Family Violence Prevention Fund, 2002).

## Substantiated Child Abuse and Neglect

In California, the odds of being a substantiated victim of child maltreatment are 2.5 times greater for African-American children than for white children (see **Figure 3.16**). Latino children are 1.3 times as likely to be the victims of substantiated maltreatment compared with white children. Nationally, the rate of substantiated victims of child maltreatment was 12.1 per 1,000

---

[8]  *The survey's objective was to obtain one-year incidence estimates of a comprehensive range of childhood victimizations across gender, race and developmental stage. A nationally representative sample of 2,030 children ages 2 to 17 years living in the United States was surveyed. Past estimates of children and youth exposure to weapon-related and physical/crime-related community violence have varied widely. Further, the types of victimization that studies have examined differ considerably, making it difficult to estimate the burden on children and adolescents (Finkelhor et al., 2005).*

FIGURE
3.15

# Children's Witnessing of Domestic Violence and Exposure to Other Forms of Violence

African-American children are 2.1 times more likely to witness domestic violence and 3 times more likely to be exposed to shootings, bombs or riots; Latino children are 2.1 times more likely to be exposed to shootings, bombs or riots.

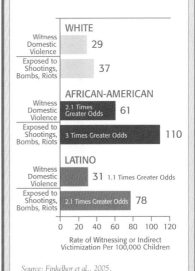

| WHITE | |
| --- | --- |
| Witness Domestic Violence | 29 |
| Exposed to Shootings, Bombs, Riots | 37 |

**AFRICAN-AMERICAN**

| | | |
| --- | --- | --- |
| Witness Domestic Violence | 2.1 Times Greater Odds | 61 |
| Exposed to Shootings, Bombs, Riots | 3 Times Greater Odds | 110 |

**LATINO**

| | | |
| --- | --- | --- |
| Witness Domestic Violence | 31 | 1.1 Times Greater Odds |
| Exposed to Shootings, Bombs, Riots | 2.1 Times Greater Odds | 78 |

0   20   40   60   80   100   120

Rate of Witnessing or Indirect Victimization Per 100,000 Children

*Source: Finkelhor et al., 2005.*

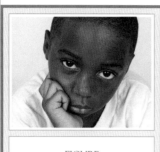

FIGURE
3.16

## Child Abuse and Neglect

African-American children are 2.5 times more likely to be substantiated victims of child maltreatment.

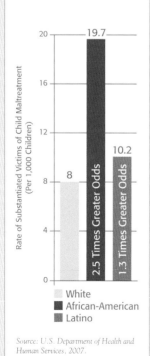

Source: U.S. Department of Health and Human Services, 2007.

children in 2005. The odds of being a victim of substantiated maltreatment were 1.8 times higher for non-Hispanic African-American children compared with non-Hispanic white children. Since 2001, the overall rate of substantiated maltreatment has declined by a small percentage (U.S. Department of Health and Human Services, 2007).

While definitions of child maltreatment vary by state, a broad definition includes physical abuse, sexual abuse, emotional abuse and neglect. Children are considered to be victims of maltreatment if a child welfare agency investigates the report and determines that there is enough evidence to substantiate the allegation. The consequences of maltreatment depend on the stage of development. For very young children, abuse and neglect can interfere with normal physical growth and development. Toddlers and school-age children who are maltreated often have trust issues, lack social skills, and exhibit behavioral problems that interfere with normal relationships. Adolescents who are maltreated are at increased risk for poor school performance and involvement with the criminal justice system. A study of 10 California counties found that children initially reported for neglect were more likely to be incarcerated in the California Youth Authority (CYA) later in life (Jonson-Reid and Barth, 2000). The rate of entry into CYA was at least two times higher for children with investigated maltreatment reports than for all children in the state. Among children investigated for maltreatment, African-American children had the highest rate of CYA entry, followed by Latino children (Jonson-Reid and Barth, 2000).

Maltreated children are also more likely to be depressed, abuse alcohol or drugs, and engage in risky sexual behavior (English, 1998). The risk factors for child maltreatment include parent, family and community characteristics. The parents and family of maltreated children are more likely to be unemployed, live in poverty, be a teen parent, use alcohol or drugs or be involved with the criminal justice system. Maltreated children are also more likely to live in neighborhoods with concentrated unemployment, poverty and crime.

This brings them into contact with authorities who are mandated reporters of child abuse and neglect and thus, the rates may be exaggerated because reporting is more likely (Hill, 2006).

## Foster Care

In California, African-American children are overrepresented in foster care, with a disproportionality index of 4.05 (see **Figure 3.17**). Nationally, African-American and Native American children are over-represented in foster care with a disproportionality index of well over two. The index represents the proportion of children in the foster care system compared with that group's overall proportion in the general population. An index number below 1.00 indicates an underrepresentation in foster care compared with that group's proportion in the general child population, while a number above 1.00 indicates an overrepresentation of children in foster care compared with that group's proportion in the general child population (GAO, 2007).

Once a report of child abuse or neglect has been substantiated, the child welfare agency determines whether it is safe for the child to remain in his or her current living situation. Children are removed from their homes and placed in foster care when they cannot be adequately protected from harm.

## Juvenile Arrest and Custody Rates

Relative to their proportion in California's youth population, African-American adolescents have juvenile arrest rates 2.5 times that of white adolescents (see **Figure 3.18**).[9] In 2005, there were almost 222,512 juvenile arrests in California, with felony arrests accounting for 27 percent of this total.[10] African Americans represent 8 percent of California's adolescent population (ages 10 to 17), but account for 17 percent of juvenile arrests. Latinos represent about 46 percent of California's adolescent population (ages 10 to 17), but account for almost half of juvenile arrests.

[9]  *Calculation of this disproportionality estimate using the data in Figure 3.18 is as follows: African Americans 17/8=2.125; Whites 28/33=0.85. Odds calculation is 2.125/0.85 = juvenile arrest rates for African-American adolescents 2.5 times that of white adolescents. Using the same method, the juvenile arrest rate for Latino adolescents is 1.2 times that of white adolescents.*

[10]  *2005 is the most recent year for which juvenile arrest data are available.*

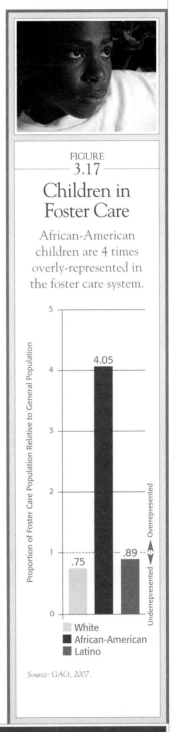

FIGURE
3.17

# Children in Foster Care

African-American children are 4 times overly-represented in the foster care system.

Proportion of Foster Care Population Relative to General Population

4.05

.75  .89

Overrepresented

Underrepresented

☐ White
■ African-American
■ Latino

*Source:* GAO, 2007.

FIGURE
3.18

# Juvenile Arrest Rates

Relative to their proportion in
the California youth population,
African-American adolescents
have juvenile arrest rates 2.5
times that of white adolescents.

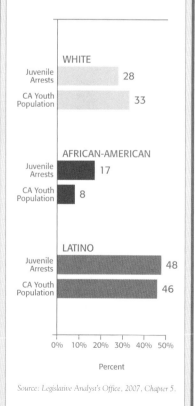

**WHITE**
Juvenile Arrests: 28
CA Youth Population: 33

**AFRICAN-AMERICAN**
Juvenile Arrests: 17
CA Youth Population: 8

**LATINO**
Juvenile Arrests: 48
CA Youth Population: 46

0%  10%  20%  30%  40%  50%
Percent

Source: Legislative Analyst's Office, 2007, Chapter 5.

FIGURE
3.19

# Custody Rates

African-American
adolescents have custody
rates 5.7 times that of
white adolescents; Latino
adolescents have custody
rates 2.1 times greater.

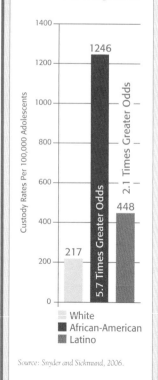

White: 217 (5.7 Times Greater Odds)
African-American: 1246
Latino: 448 (2.1 Times Greater Odds)

Custody Rates Per 100,000 Adolescents

■ White
■ African-American
■ Latino

Source: Snyder and Sickmund, 2006.

African-American adolescents have custody rates 5.7 times that of white adolescents, while Latino adolescents have rates 2.1 times higher (see **Figure 3.19**). In California, custody rates are highest for African-American youth. For every 100,000 African-American juveniles living in California, 1,246 are in custody (Snyder and Sickmund, 2006).

In California, Latino juvenile offenders are more than 3 times as likely (and African-American juvenile offenders nearly 2 times as likely) as other incarcerated youth to be represented among the California's Department of Juvenile Justice (DJJ) institutions and camps (CDCR, 2008b).[11]

## Lifetime Likelihood of Ever Going to Prison

Nationally, African-American men are 5.5 times more likely than white men to go to prison in their lifetimes (see **Figure 3.20**). The odds of Latino men going to prison during their lifetimes are 2.9 times higher than for white men (Bonczar, 2003). Overall, 1 in 3 African-American men, 1 in 6 Latino men, and 1 in 17 white men are expected to go to prison during their lifetimes (assuming current trends in incarceration rates) (Bonczar, 2003).

[11] In 2007, there were 2,115 juvenile offenders in California's Department of Juvenile Justice (DJJ) institutions and camps, mostly for violent offenses. Fifty-four percent were Hispanic, 30 percent were African-American, and 12 percent were white (with the remaining 4 percent including other ethnic groups). The average age was 19.8 years and 95 percent were male. The mean length of stay was 33.6 months (CDCR, 2007a).

Changes in first incarceration and mortality rates between 1974 and 2001 have had different impacts on lifetime incarceration depending on race and ethnicity. The likelihood of African-American men going to prison over their lifetimes has increased more than any other group, with Latino men experiencing the second-largest increase (Bonczar, 2003). Based on current rates of first incarceration, an estimated 6.7 percent of African-American men in the United States will enter state or federal prison by age 20, compared with 3 percent of Latino men and less than 1 percent of white men (Bonczar, 2003).

## Disproportional Representation in the Prison Population

In California, African Americans are disproportionately represented in the prison population. Although African Americans make up 6.7 percent of the state population, they represent 29 percent of the state prison population. Overall, African Americans and Latinos represent approximately 43 percent of California's population, but 68 percent of its prison population (CDCR, 2008b; U.S. Census Bureau, 2008).

African Americans are overrepresented in the prison population with a disproportionality index of 4.33; whites are underrepresented with a disproportionality index of 0.67 (see **Figure 3.21**). For the prison population, the disproportionality index represents the proportion of African Americans or Latinos in the prison population when compared with each group's overall proportion in the general population.

## Incarceration Rate

In California, the disproportional representation of minorities in prisons is also evident when examining incarceration rates (see **Figure 3.22**). Among adult men, the odds of an African-American man being incarcerated are 6.7 times higher than for a white man. The odds for a Latino man are 1.5 times higher.

FIGURE
3.20

## Lifetime Likelihood of Going to Prison

African-American men are 5.5 times more likely to go to prison during their lifetime; Latino men are 2.9 times more likely.

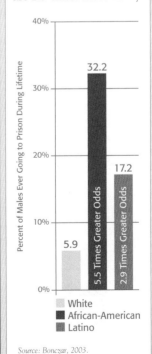

*Source: Bonczar, 2003.*

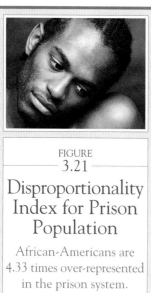

FIGURE
3.21

# Disproportionality Index for Prison Population

African-Americans are 4.33 times over-represented in the prison system.

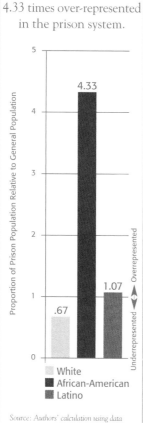

Source: Authors' calculation using data from CDCR, 2008b and U.S. Census Bureau, 2008.

FIGURE
3.22

# Incarceration Rate

African-American men are 6.7 times more likely to be incarcerated.

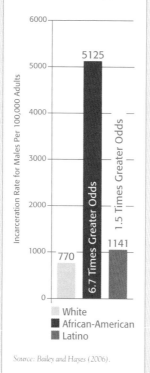

Source: Bailey and Hayes (2006).

Between 1990 and 2005, California's prison population grew three times faster than the general adult population (Bailey and Hayes, 2006). By the end of 2007, the state prison population was 171,568 (CDCR, 2008b).[12] The racial and ethnic composition of California prisons has changed dramatically over the past 40 years. Between 1964 and 1984, African Americans and Latinos were incarcerated at higher numbers, while the number of white inmates has increased only somewhat (Petersilia, 2006).

In 2007, Latinos constituted the largest group in the prison system at 39 percent, followed by African Americans at 29 percent and whites at 29 percent. Thirteen and a half percent of all inmates were under 25 years of age; 93 percent of the state prison population was male and the mean age for males was 37 years old (CDCR, 2008b).

## Children with Incarcerated Parents

Nationally, African-American children are almost nine times more likely, and Latino children are more than three times more likely, than white children to have a parent in prison (see **Figure 3.23**). Overall, more than half of the 1.4 million adults incarcerated in state and federal prisons are parents of minor children (Travis, McBride, and Solomon, 2005).

[12] Refers to the prison institution population on December 31, 2007 (CDCR, 2008b).

An estimated 856,000 California children—approximately 1 in 9—have a parent currently involved in the adult criminal justice system.[13] Based on findings from the 2004 Survey of Inmates in State and Federal Correctional Facilities, 50 percent of African-American inmates, 60 percent of Latino inmates, and 53 percent of white inmates in state prison have children under the age of 18 years (U.S. Department of Justice, Bureau of Justice Statistics , 2007).

The imprisonment of parents disrupts parent-child relationships, alters the networks of familial support, and places new burdens on governmental services such as schools, foster care, adoption agencies and youth-serving organizations (Travis, McBride and Solomon, 2005). Children of incarcerated parents are more likely to exhibit low self-esteem, depression, emotional withdrawal from friends and family and inappropriate or disruptive behavior at home and in school, and they are at increased risk of future delinquency and/or criminal behavior (Travis and Waul, 2003).

### Firearms-Related Death Rates

In California, the firearms-related death rate for young African-American men (ages 15 to 24) is more than ten times that of young white men (see **Figure 3.24**). Young Latino men have a

FIGURE
3.23

## Children with Incarcerated Parents

African-American children are 8.8 times more likely to have an incarcerated parent; Latino children are 3.3 times more likely.

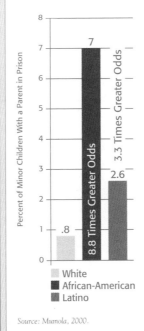

Source: Mumola, 2000.

FIGURE
3.24

## Firearms-Related Death Rate

Young African-American men have a firearms-related death rate 10.1 times that of young white men; young Latino men have a rate that is 3.3 times greater.

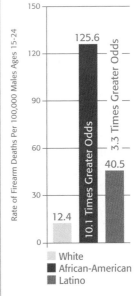

Source: California Department of Health Care Services, 2007a. Note: Age-adjusted death rates are per 100,000.

[13] Calculation of 1 in 9 children is based on U.S. Census Bureau, March 1999 Current Population Survey. There were about 9.8 million children ages 0–18 in California in 1999 (Simmons, 2000).

FIGURE
3.25

## Homicide-Related Death Rate

Young African-American men have a homicide death rate 16.4 times that of young white men; young Latino men have a homicide death rate 5.1 times greater.

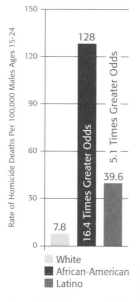

Source: California Department of Health Care Services, 2007b. Note: Age-adjusted death rates are per 100,000.

firearms-related death rate more than three times greater than that of young white men (15 to 24 years).

### Homicide-Related Death Rates

Homicide is the sixth leading cause of death among African-American men and the seventh leading cause of death among Latino men in California (Lee and McConville, 2007).[14] Young African-American men (15 to 24 years) have a homicide death rate of more than 16 times that of young white men (see **Figure 3.25**). Young Latino men have a homicide death rate 5 times greater than that of young white men.

## Ready to Learn

In the ready to learn outcome area, we examined indicators related to educational attainment and performance. **Table 3.4** shows indicators in five areas—high school completion rates, student achievement (reading proficiency in grades 4 and 8), student achievement (math proficiency in grades 4 and 8), school suspension, and grade retention—where are the odds are two times or greater. Other indicators in this area, which included preschool attendance and absenteeism, did not exhibit odds greater than 2.0 times.

TABLE
3.4

### Ready to Learn Outcome Indicators with Odds for Boys and Men of Color Greater Than Twice What They Are for White Boys and Men

| | |
|---|---|
| High school completion | School suspension |
| Student achievement: Math proficiency | Grade retention |
| Student achievement: Reading proficiency | |

[14] For adult African-American men (25 years and older), heart disease drives much of the mortality disadvantage followed by homicide. Time period of the death certificate data is 2000–2002 (Lee and McConville, 2007).

## High School Completion

The returns to education have grown over the last two decades: in 2006 the median earnings of male year-round, full-time workers with a bachelor's degree were $66,930; those with a high school degree, $37,030; and those with some high school $27,650 (U.S. Department of Education, 2007b). In addition to accounting for earnings differences, high school graduation status is also linked to improvements in health status (Smith, 2005) and children's outcomes (Currie and Morretti, 2003).

African-American Californians over age 25 are nearly twice as likely to be without a high school diploma as whites, while Latinos in California are almost seven times as likely to be without a high school degree (see **Figure 3.26**). This extremely large gap for Latinos is explained in part by the differences in educational attainment between native-born and other citizens. In California, about nine out of ten native-born U.S. citizens have a high school degree, compared with only half of noncitizens and three-quarters of naturalized citizens (California Department of Finance, 2007b).

## Student Achievement: Math and Reading Proficiency

California children perform worse than the national average on most measures of academic achievement. Here, we present results from 2006 National Assessment of Educational Progress, or NAEP, is the longest-running and most widely used set of nationally representative achievement tests. We show the percentage of students scoring below basic proficiency for reading and math \in grades 4 and 8 for California in **Figures 3.27** and **3.28**. In general, white students are least likely to score below basic proficiency on all four sets of tests.

One way that California differs from the rest of the country is that for the grade 4 tests, Latinos are the most likely to score below basic proficiency, while in the rest of the country, African Americans are most likely to score below basic proficiency. However, for the grade 8 tests, the race and ethnicity

FIGURE
3.26

# No High School Degree

Latino adults are 6.7 times more likely to have less than a high school degree; African-American adults are 1.9 times more likely to have less than a high school degree.

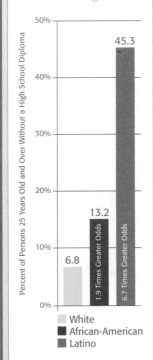

Source: *California Department of Finance, 2007b.*

FIGURE
3.27

## Below Proficiency on Reading Test

African-American *fourth graders* are 2.2 times more likely to score below proficient on the Grade 4 NAEP Reading Test; Latino *fourth graders* are 2.3 times more likely; African-American *eighth graders* are 2.4 times more likely to score below proficient on the Grade 8 NAEP Reading Test; Latino *eighth graders* are 2.3 times more likely.

**WHITE**
Grade 4 — 26
Grade 8 — 22

**AFRICAN-AMERICAN**
Grade 4 — 2.2 Times Greater Odds — 58
Grade 8 — 2.4 Times Greater Odds — 53

**LATINO**
Grade 4 — 2.3 Times Greater Odds — 61
Grade 8 — 2.3 Times Greater Odds — 50

0%  20%  40%  60%
Percent Below Basic Proficiency on NAEP Reading Test

Source: U.S. Department of Education, 2007c.

FIGURE
3.28

## Below Proficiency on Math Test

African-American *fourth graders* are 3.5 times more likely to score below proficient on the Grade 4 NAEP Reading Test; Latino *fourth graders* are 3.6 times more likely; African-American *eighth graders* are 2.8 times more likely to score below proficient on the Grade 8 NAEP Reading Test; Latino *eighth graders* are 2.5 times more likely.

**WHITE**
Grade 4 — 12
Grade 8 — 22

**AFRICAN-AMERICAN**
Grade 4 — 3.5 Times Greater Odds — 42
Grade 8 — 2.8 Times Greater Odds — 62

**LATINO**
Grade 4 — 3.6 Times Greater Odds — 43
Grade 8 — 2.5 Times Greater Odds — 56

0%  15%  30%  45%  60%  75%
Percent Below Basic Proficiency on NAEP Math Test

Source: U.S. Department of Education, 2007c.

patterns in California mirror those in the rest of the nation, with African Americans being the most likely to score below basic proficiency.

For both African-American and Latino students, the gaps between their scores and those of whites are larger for math than for reading. These gaps shrink between fourth grade and eighth grade for math, but for reading, they grow slightly for African Americans and stay the same for Latinos.

### School Suspension

Recent data for California on suspensions are not available, but national data show that African-American male students were nearly two and a half times as likely to be suspended in 2000 as white students (see **Figure 3.29**). The difference between the suspension rate of Latino students and white students is small, with Latino male students being only 1.2 times more likely to be suspended in 2000. Suspension is considered to be an indicator of a lack of learning, both because it is assumed that students who are disruptive at school are not able to concentrate on learning and because students are not learning when they are absent from school. Indeed, school suspension has been shown to be predictive of dropping out of school (Wehlage et al., 1989; Jimerson, 1999).

## Grade Retention

Grade retention is a clear indicator of lack of school success, although data show that grade retention is associated with high school graduation. In 2004, only 4 percent of individuals who completed high school had repeated a grade compared with 21 percent of high school dropouts (U.S. Department of Education, 2007a). Separate data for male and female students by race and Latino origin are not available for recent years. However, national data from 2004 indicate that male students are more than twice as likely to repeat a grade as female students, with 13 percent of male students having ever been retained compared to 6 percent of female students (U.S. Department of Education, 2007a). The same data show that African-American students are twice as likely to have ever been retained in grade, and Latino students are 1.1 times more likely (see **Figure 3.30**), as white students.

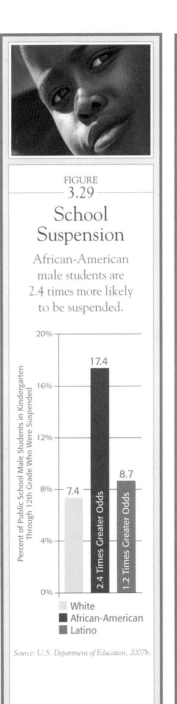

FIGURE
3.29

## School Suspension

African-American male students are 2.4 times more likely to be suspended.

Percent of Public School Male Students in Kindergarten Through 12th Grade Who Were Suspended

- White: 7.4
- African-American: 17.4 (2.4 Times Greater Odds)
- Latino: 8.7 (1.2 Times Greater Odds)

Source: U.S. Department of Education, 2007b.

FIGURE
3.30

## Grade Retention

African-American students are 2.0 times more likely to have ever been retained in grade.

Percent of 16-19 Year Olds Ever Retained in Grade

- White: 8.1
- African-American: 16.1 (2 Times Greater Odds)
- Latino: 9.2 (1.1 Times Greater Odds)

Source: U.S. Department of Education, 2007a.

While school suspension and grade retention are correlated with a lack of success in school, there are questions about whether the policies guiding these outcomes are objective or based on different norms or other factors. Analysis demonstrates that social and economic background explains many of the differences across groups in grade retention (Hauser, Brown, and Prosser, 2004).

## Geographic Concentration of Disadvantage: Neighborhood Effects

Above, we presented the odds findings at the state level, which can mask the greater odds boys or young men of color may face living in areas of concentrated poverty. For example, in the area of achievement, some studies have reported a link between neighborhood low-socioeconomic status and poor educational outcomes (Leventhal and Brooks-Gunn, 2004). In addition, there is growing evidence that neighborhood low-socioeconomic status is associated with negative behavioral and emotional outcomes and crime and delinquency (Leventhal and Brooks-Gunn, 2004).

In addition, there are neighborhood contextual factors that contribute to the development of boys and men of color. This is important because boys and men of color are likely to experience neighborhood conditions that further exacerbate the depressed trajectories that result from their individual-level disadvantages such as family poverty and low maternal education. For example, studies have documented that African-American children tend to attend schools of lower quality (Fryer and Levitt, 2004) and receive lower quality health care (Fiscella et al., 2000). We briefly summarize the theories and empirical research literature on the influence of neighborhood characteristics on the development and well-being of children.

Consensus supports the idea that neighborhood effects on adolescent development are largely indirect, operating through individual-, family-, and community-level processes (Leventhal and Brooks-Gunn, 2004).

Leventhal and Brooks-Gunn (2004) proposed a framework for conceptualizing how neighborhoods influence adolescent development using three complementary models. Their first model focuses on institutional resources, with the quality, quantity, affordability and diversity of community resources—such as schools, health and social services, recreational and social programs and employment—mediating neighborhood effects. For example, Furstenberg (2001) found that the extent of prosocial activities, such as the presence of social and recreational activities, varies across neighborhoods and is linked to problem behavior. Scott et al. (2007) found that accessibility of schools on weekends is lower in lower socioeconomic status and minority neighborhoods. Moore and Diez Roux (2006) noted that predominately lower-income and minority communities have fewer available chain supermarkets compared with higher-income and predominately white communities.

Leventhal and Brooks-Gunn's (2004) second model focuses on relationships and ties, asserting that parental attributes, social networks and behavior, as well as the home environment characteristics, moderate or diffuse neighborhood influences. For example, Cohen et al. (2006) found that in less close-knit neighborhoods, adolescents were more likely to be overweight, even after controlling for other factors. In terms of adolescents' own relationships and ties, Stiffman et al. (1999) found that when adolescents received support from family and peers it appeared to buffer the association between neighborhood problems and their mental health.

The third model, norms and collective efficacy, addresses the extent to which community formal and informal institutions monitor residents' behavior (especially peer groups) and physical threats to residents account for neighborhood effects. Community formal and information institutions act as regulatory mechanisms. For example, Jones et al. (2005) found that monitoring by parents, friends and neighborhoods is higher in neighborhoods where violence is perceived to be high. Ford and Beveridge (2006) found that the presence of a visible drug market in a neighborhood was significantly associated with crime victimization rates. Cohen, Inagami, and Finch (2008) found that the higher prevalence of alcohol outlets, such as liquor stores or bars, was negatively associated with community trust and willingness of residents to intervene in social situations (or collective efficacy).

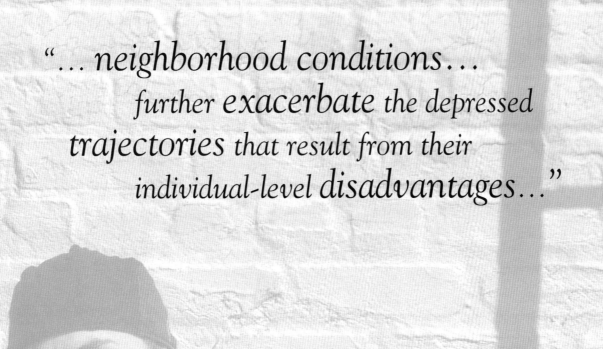

"… neighborhood conditions…
further exacerbate the depressed
trajectories that result from their
individual-level disadvantages…"

# Addressing Disparities Faced by Boys and Men of Color in California

*The conceptual framework in Chapter Two illustrates that there are multiple pathways through which factors in the physical, social, economic and family domains contribute to individual well-being. A growing body of research suggests that the disparities in odds for boys and men of color that we summarize here are largely the result of a cumulative set of factors—including adverse socioeconomic conditions and unequal access to health care, quality education, adequate housing and employment—which, together, play large roles in generating these disparities.*

Given this broader context, what can policymakers, government agencies, philanthropic foundations, community organizations and service providers do to improve the life chances of boys and men of color in California?

Here, we present some examples of approaches for reducing the disparities, selected because they have research evidence demonstrating their effectiveness and because they illustrate some key points. We ground the discussion of those approaches in terms of the conceptual model we represented in Chapter Two, which entails putting the approaches within the context of the four levels of the framework: macro level, community level, interpersonal level, and individual level. Our discussion is not intended to be a comprehensive review of all strategies for reducing the disparities for boys and men of color, but rather we provide a framework that may serve as a foundation for improving those odds.

## Reducing the Disparities: The Macro Level

Macro-level factors include aspects of the natural environment, macro-social factors such as historical conditions and social institutions, and underlying inequalities. These macro-level factors are clearly the most firmly rooted ones, and many are either immutable—as in the case of topography—or entail long-term modification of social norms—as in the case of altering expectations about gender roles. However, some macro-level factors are more readily modifiable, such as legal codes, which are the purview of policymakers, who can effect change by addressing inequalities in the systems that provide employment, educational and service opportunities.

When we reviewed the recommendations from commissions and expert panels that addressed macro-level factors that contribute to disparities, these recommendations often stressed identifying and addressing inequities in the systems that provide employment, educational and service opportunities. These included changing laws that introduced disparities, modifying structural anomalies, and providing more of a feedback loop between community members and the systems that served them. An example of a recommendation in the safety outcome area that involved a legal code change is one made by the Dellums Commission to modify sentencing codes that impose relatively harsh mandatory incarceration terms for crack cocaine offenders relative to powder cocaine offenders (Dellums Commission, 2006). One of the overarching themes from these commissions and panels is the value of examining data to identify the points in the system that could be improved. As discussed above, an important example related to data is the opportunity to improve the quantity and quality of data on the large population of Asian boys and men in California, an issue we faced in conducting this study.

An example of a policy-level approach for addressing factors that contribute to disparities in foster care is in the area of legal guardianship. In its report, *African-American Children in Foster Care* (2007), The U.S. Government

Accounting Office (GAO) recommended that Congress consider amending federal law to allow federal reimbursement for legal guardianship in much the same way it is currently done for adoption. This would assist states in increasing the number of homes available for the permanent placement of African-American and other children from foster care. To enhance states' ability to reduce the proportion of African-American children in foster care, the GAO also recommended that the Secretary of Health and Human Services help states understand the nature and extent of disproportionality in their child welfare systems by, for example, encouraging states to regularly track state and local data on the ethnic and racial disproportionality of children in foster care.

Prisoner reentry is another area where policy-level approaches can help improve links between communities and state systems, and improve the use of data analysis for identifying opportunities. The California Department of Corrections and Rehabilitation (CDCR) Expert Panel conducted an assessment of California's adult prison and parole programs aimed at reducing recidivism. In its *Report to the California State Legislature: A Roadmap for Effective Offender Programming* (CDCR, 2007b), the expert panel put forth a set of recommendations for improving programming, the parole system, and reentry resources to help in transitioning ex-offenders back into the community. One key recommendation was that the CDCR develop and strengthen its formal partnerships with community stakeholders on reentry, including establishing interagency steering committees at the community and state levels to coordinate the transition of services for those returning from prison back to their communities.

## Reducing the Disparities: The Community Level

Moving to the community level, more opportunities exist to make changes that are likely to improve the odds for men and boys of color. In fact, the public health community increasingly recognizes the "social determinants" of health as primary predictors of individual outcomes. This theory of health determination emphasizes the importance of socioeconomic status, education level and other "non-biological" conditions. Among the community-level factors in the conceptual framework, this would include access to *health-promoting* services, such as parks, or *health-robbing* experiences, such as relentless community violence, exposure to environmental toxins and poor school quality. In addition to the people who reside in communities, policymakers at the national, state, and local levels impact these community-level factors, as do decision-makers from other sectors, such as the faith-based sector and the non-profit sector.

Thus, actions to improve community-level factors that promote good outcomes or reduce bad ones for men and boys of color encompass a vast spectrum of activities and may use a variety of strategies to address numerous challenges. In Los Angeles County, the Child Care Planning Committee and the Policy Roundtable on Child Care work to modify zoning laws in the county so that more children of color will have access to licensed child care settings. To address disparities in environmental exposure, Washington, D.C. lawmakers undertook pollution-reduction measures, such as enforcing anti-idling ordinances and regulating small-source emissions, and announced reductions in the number of unhealthy air quality days in the district by nearly half (District of Columbia Department of the Environment, 2006). The District had the highest rates of asthma in the country, and reducing unhealthy air quality days was expected to improve asthma outcomes for children, most of whom are children of color (District of Columbia Department of Health, 2000). Multnomah County, Oregon addressed the problem that youth of color were disproportionately represented in its juvenile system by implementing a series of reforms that included establishing a Disproportionate Minority Confinement Committee that relied on objective analysis of data to achieve racial parity by 2000 (Dellums Commission, 2006).

Community partnerships—which involve mobilizing resources across community institutions in a coordinated effort to address a particular issue—are increasingly recognized as a promising community-level approach to addressing complex social problems, such as racial disparities, that have multi-faceted causes and cross the lines of any one organization (Edwards and Stern, 1998). The advantages of community partnerships may include increased efficiency gained by eliminating duplicative services, improving service coordination and integration, and modifying community norms and values to promote healthy behaviors (Bracht, 1995). In fact, agencies and organizations that fund prevention services increasingly require implementation through community partnerships (Center for Substance Abuse Prevention, 1995).

One example of a comprehensive community initiative is the Ford Foundation's Neighborhood and Family Initiative. Implemented in four cities over a five-year period, the initiative sought to develop and integrate social, physical and economic efforts throughout the community, with a strong focus on community involvement in the change process (Chaskin et al., 2001).

An example of a community partnership in California comes from the after-school care arena. Stone Soup Child Care has created community collaboratives to provide after-school care to more than 4,000 primarily elementary school-age children of color in mostly low-performing school districts in California. The sites partner with schools to access unused facilities and equipment after school, and with a network of funders that includes parents, businesses and philanthropic organizations. Staff members include parents, volunteers and Stone Soup staff, and each site implements curricula and programs that reflect the needs and preferences of that community (Stone Soup Child Care Programs, no date).

While a comprehensive catalog of the many approaches to improve the community context of the life course for men and boys is beyond the scope of this report, we refer readers to a rich literature on social determinants of

health and community health initiatives in such landmark reports as the Dellums Commission report (2006) and *The Social Determinants of Health: Developing an Evidence Base for Political Action* final report to the World Health Organization (Kelly et al., 2007).

## Reducing the Disparities: The Interpersonal and Individual Levels

The most proximate approach generally taken to improve outcomes at the individual level is to implement "programs," which operate by changing the intra- and interpersonal factors that affect individual outcomes. Programs are typically a coordinated set of planned activities, often with prescribed curricula that are designed to improve health behaviors, strengthen family assets, or promote resilience to stressors. Programs often target a specific individual outcome—such as a particular substance abuse program designed to reduce cigarette smoking—and typically work by improving participants' skills or knowledge to improve health behaviors or improve access to health inputs.

The impact of programs on participant outcomes can often be evaluated using rigorous statistical approaches, such as randomized control trials. A recent trend in social programs has been to favor or even require the use of "evidence-based" programs. The latter term refers to programs that have met specific guidelines about the scientific evidence required to demonstrate effectiveness (Hallfors, Pankratz & Hartman, 2007). Only a fraction of implemented programs are ever evaluated, and only a handful of these meets the strict standards for being designated "evidence-based."

Despite this, there is a surprisingly large set of programs targeted toward improving the indicators highlighted in this report that have met these standards. For example, in the area of alcohol, tobacco and other drug prevention, a recent survey of state offices found that they consulted nearly a dozen lists of evidence-based effective programs (Hallfors, Pankratz, and Hartman, 2007). Some of these are targeted toward boys and men of color, but many of them serve boys and girls, and many do not target specific racial or ethnic groups.

As an example, in **Table 4.1** we show the number of programs on one evidence-based program list—the Promising Practices Network (PPN)[15]— related to four indicators where our analysis above showed large disparities for people of color. There are at least half a dozen "model program" or "best practices" review projects; we use PPN for our example because it covers the full range of topics addressed in this report (most other examples cover only one topic) and because PPN links to all these other projects' reviews and so has, in fact, incorporated the entire set of information that meets its evidence criteria.

TABLE
4.1

## Examples of Indicators and Number of Programs Listed on Promising Practices Network Website

| Indicator | Number of Programs Listed |
|---|---|
| Children and youth not engaging in violent behavior or displaying serious conduct problems | 63 |
| Children not experiencing physical, psychological or emotional abuse | 8 |
| Students performing at grade level or meeting state curriculum standards | 46 |
| Youths abstaining from sexual activity or not engaging in risky sexual behavior | 12 |

Note: PPN Web site (Promising Practices Network, 2008a) as of March 6, 2008.

[15] PPN is a collaboration between the RAND Corporation and public and private organizations to systematically review scientific evidence related to improving outcomes for children and families. PPN produces a website that presents the findings from these reviews, including a section on programs that have met predesignated standards for scientific rigor (Promising Practices Network, 2008b). We refer the reader to the website for a complete list of programs that have been reviewed by this particular "best practices" project. In addition to the programs listed on this site, there are other programs that have demonstrated effectiveness but may not be posted on PPN because they address indicators outside the scope of the project or because they are currently under peer review.

This table shows that for these four indicators, the PPN has identified a substantial number of programs with evaluation findings demonstrating the potential to improve participants' outcomes. In sum, this brief description of programs to improve outcomes for young people argues that a large number of programs exist that are shown to have the potential to improve outcomes for some of the very indicators in areas that exhibit large disparities for boys and men of color.

Of course, implementing evidence-based "model programs" is not always practical, because communities vary in their resources, needs and cultural contexts. As a result, many individual-level interventions adapt the practices of model programs to their own context. We consider "practices" to be the activities and features customarily incorporated into the approaches and interventions, and these are often the core features of the activity that are believed to contribute to its effectiveness in improving outcomes. Practices are much more difficult to evaluate, because there is less information in the scientific literature on which to base effective practice guidelines. In many social service arenas, such as substance abuse prevention and home visiting, the first generation of research has demonstrated whether particular program models can improve participant outcomes, and a second generation of research just getting underway is attempting to "unpack" the services those programs provide to identify what practices are required to improve outcomes.

In surveying the 175 programs listed on the PPN, it is evident that some practices are pervasive among evidence-based programs. The following list is not meant to be exhaustive, but rather to provide a sample of some of the types of practices that are widely represented in effective approaches for improving children and youth outcomes.

- **Mentoring.** More than a dozen programs listed on PPN use mentoring as one of the primary practices in improving outcomes for young people. From massive nationwide programs to small-scale model programs,

programs built around mentoring have been shown to increase the number of youths graduating from high school, reduce conduct problems, improve performance on measures of achievement, and improve other outcomes highlighted above. Evidence-based mentoring programs operating in California include Big Brothers/Big Sisters, Achievement for Latinos Through Academic Success, and Multi-Dimensional Treatment Foster Care.

- **Infusion of Behavioral Health Services.** Many of the effective approaches to improving the well-being of young people recognize the need for a coupling of services that target a particular outcome and behavioral health services. Programs that are specifically designed to target substance abuse, gang involvement or violence prevention are increasingly likely to include components to address behavioral health issues ranging from post-traumatic stress to anxiety to depression. One example of a California-based program that has been evaluated and meets the strict standards for being designated "evidence-based" is Cognitive-Behavioral Intervention for Trauma in Schools (CBITS)—a school-based intervention to help children traumatized by violence improve behavioral, emotional and schooling outcomes. In Los Angeles, public middle schools with mostly Latino students received CBITS from school-based mental health clinicians. The evaluation of CBITS found that students from economically disadvantaged neighborhoods who participated in the program had significantly less post-traumatic stress symptoms, depression and psychosocial dysfunction (Jaycox et al., 2002). Another example is Multisystemic Therapy (MST), an intensive, family-based treatment approach for improving the behavior of serious juvenile offenders (Curtis, Ronin, and Borduin, 2004).

- **Comprehensive or Integrated Services.** Another hallmark of many approaches is the emphasis on services that cut across outcome areas or bureaucratic functional lines. For example, early childhood intervention services are most often provided using a combination of preschool,

*"… participants significantly improved their academic performance and overall behavior… twice as likely to complete the terms of their probation."*

home visiting, early screening and case management, rather than by using one of these alone (Karoly et al., 2005). One example from the field of juvenile justice is the provision of wraparound case management services designed to keep delinquent youth at home and out of institutions where possible. In California, the Repeat Offender Prevention Program (ROPP)—a demonstration program from 1996 to 2002—provided wraparound services to at-risk youth (ages 8 to 15 years), including first-time offenders, youth with chronic truancy problems, and gang-involved and substance-abusing youth. Evaluation of the ROPP found that program participants significantly improved their academic performance and overall behavior. They were also almost twice as likely to complete the terms of their probation as youth from a comparison group (California Board of Corrections, 2002).

- **Learning Using Non-Didactic Approaches.** A final example of a practice that is represented among many of the effective program models is the recognition that participant learning takes place through experiential approaches, such as role-playing, rather than through didactic approaches, such as straight lecturing. Examples of this come from the substance-abuse prevention arena, where California interventions, such as *Keepin' It R.E.A.L.* (Promising Practices Network, 2008c) and *Project ALERT* (Promising Practices Network, 2008d) focus on practicing resistance skills, learning the benefits of not using alcohol, tobacco, and other drugs, and recognizing that most people do not use drugs.

### What The California Endowment Is Doing

Some other examples of practices in these four areas include ongoing programs funded by The California Endowment that address some of the safety and health issues identified above for boys and men of color. Some of these programs have yet to be, or are in the process of being, evaluated, and are summarized in the following pages.

## Sample of Relevant Programs Funded by The California Endowment

| Program Name | What It Does |
|---|---|
| **Homeboy Industries Mental Health Education and Treatment Assistance Services** | Homeboy Industries—an innovative and widely respected gang-intervention organization in Los Angeles—provides jobs and job training to at-risk youth and young adults in its small businesses, including a bakery and silkscreen shop, but also incorporates much needed mental health services.<br><br>As much as jobs may be the key, employment doesn't exist in a vacuum. From its start in 1988, Homeboy Industries has worked to address the many challenges facing those trying to move from gang-involved life to positive roles in the community, providing services as disparate as tattoo removal and legal assistance.<br><br>Another key need is mental health. Up to 70 percent of gang-involved youth have mental health issues, such as post-traumatic stress disorder and depression; many also suffer from addiction. A grant from The California Endowment has helped Homeboy Industries expand its mental health services.<br><br>In the organization's newly built headquarters—in a gang-neutral location that helps broaden the organization's reach beyond its East Los Angeles origins—The California Endowment is helping to fund five private counseling rooms and a large room for group sessions. The grant also supports full-time staffers to provide mental health and substance abuse counseling to all comers; those participating in Homeboy Industries' job programs receive intensive case-management services. |
| **San Diego Second Chance Re-entry Advocacy Project** | From 1986 to 2006, California's prison population grew from 59,000 to 173,000 inmates. What happens to those inmates when they are released back into communities is the concern of Second Chance, a grassroots nonprofit based in San Diego. Second Chance provides a set of comprehensive and integrated services to help released inmates adjust to reentry.<br><br>Founded in 1993, the organization creates healthy environments for former prisoners in San Diego. Ex-inmates faced with re-integrating into their communities are confronted with an array of |

| continued | |
|---|---|
| **Program Name** | **What It Does** |
| **San Diego Second Chance Re-entry Advocacy Project** (continued) | challenges, ranging from employment to housing to mental wellness. Second Chance's holistic approach, which it calls the PREP Program, combines pre-release outreach with drug- and alcohol-free housing, mental health counseling, and job training and placement after release. While just 20–30 percent of parolees in San Diego find and keep jobs, that ratio is 80 percent for PREP graduates, who also show lowered rates of depression and recidivism. |
| **Youth UpRising PeaceMaking Program** | For 10 years, Youth UpRising has worked in Oakland to provide positive opportunities for at-risk youth. The organization's 25,000-square-foot facility provides a set of cross-cutting, integrative services, including a media arts center, dance studio, café, classrooms and a health clinic. But the organization decided it needed to do more. So with a grant from The California Endowment, it's taking it to the streets with the PeaceMaking Program.<br><br>The PeaceMaking Program, now focused on East Oakland, builds on individual relationships, moving from sidewalks to schoolyards to homes. Its one-on-one interactions are designed to build trust and positive change in a community that has been plagued by violence. To help prevent violence, the organization provides mentoring services and referrals to mental health resources, job training programs and educational opportunities. Also a key activity is the organization's focus on intervening in the patterns of gang violence—an activity it enacts using a fully realized mediation system that includes conversation, commitment and formal conflict resolution. Each year, the PeaceMaking team logs thousands of hours of street outreach.<br><br>The California Endowment's grant also supports developing two communications strategies, one focused on at-risk youth and one focused on the media. To reach young people, the organization is developing multimedia messages designed to build positive perceptions of community, loyalty, honor, and success that will be circulated through culturally appropriate venues. At the same time, it is also |

| continued | |
|---|---|
| **Program Name** | **What It Does** |
| **Youth UpRising PeaceMaking Program** (continued) | devising a comprehensive press strategy aimed at raising the issue of violence reduction in the media.<br><br>The work of the PeaceMaking Program goes through an annual evaluation, helping to memorialize its successes. Youth UpRising plans to expand these successes, not just across Oakland, but also to such nearby cities as Stockton and Richmond. |
| **The Mentoring Center** | Mentoring comes in many forms at the Mentoring Center. In its 16 years serving mentoring programs and providing direct mentoring services in the Bay Area, the Center has touched more than 25,000 lives.<br><br>In its efforts to reach some of the area's most at-risk youth, The Mentoring Center has created a focused group-mentoring program known as Positive Minds Group—or PMG—and has taken it on location. With a grant from The California Endowment, PMG On Location will eventually be fully implemented at three schools. These schools— including one that takes students who have been expelled from others in the region—set aside class time so their students can participate.<br><br>With dynamic facilitators using an established curriculum, PMG On Location provides intentional, structured, and corrective intervention for youth who are not just "at risk"of destructive behaviors but who have become immersed in them. Over about 10 weeks, this transformative mentoring aims to change attitudes that lead toward destructive behavior. Group sessions improve self-esteem and self-awareness, build character and improve life skills. The California Endowment supports expanded services that include peer mentors and a case manager who meet one-on-one with all participants to provide referrals to mental health and other needed services.<br><br>The lack of educational achievement is one of the greatest indicators of future incarceration. The Mentoring Center's PMG On Location is specifically designed to reach those young people who are the most at risk of dropping out of the educational system and to revive their desire to achieve. |

## continued

| Program Name | What It Does |
|---|---|
| **National League of Cities Institute's Gang Prevention Network** | The effects of gang violence are so widespread that they may be impossible to fully calculate. In the last 15 years, 10,000 lives were lost to gang violence in California, while in 2004, gangs were at the root of 75 percent of homicides statewide. Gang violence creates physically unsafe environments that deeply affect the psychological and emotional health of individuals and weaken the communities in which they live.<br><br>To help keep youth on track for positive social, educational and emotional development, the National League of Cities (NLC) has launched a coordinated effort to reduce gang violence in 13 cities in California. With support from The California Endowment, this effort—the Gang Prevention Network—brings together civic and community leaders to develop and promote new approaches to reducing gang violence—approaches that innovatively and comprehensively combine intervention, enforcement and prevention.<br><br>The cities range from Fresno to San Diego, Sacramento to Oxnard, and vary widely in available resources and existing capacities. The Gang Prevention Network has faced this challenge—as well as such issues as standardizing data and establishing common benchmarks—head-on, working together collaboratively. Community leaders have been able to share best practices and lessons learned, take away models for successful programs, and build a common agenda for addressing gang violence.<br><br>Making sure this agenda is heard and understood in the places where it might have the most impact—with state and federal decision-makers—is a Gang Prevention Network goal. By considering the problem of gang violence comprehensively—looking to both grandmothers and governors to play a part in addressing it—the Gang Prevention Network hopes to make a real difference in creating safer communities. |

| continued | |
| --- | --- |
| **Program Name** | **What It Does** |
| **Healthy Returns Initiative** | Young offenders who end up in California's juvenile justice system often start out at a disadvantage: Many have been foster kids or have struggled with mental health issues and other disorders, including addiction. One of the few positive aspects of their detention is that it enables the juvenile justice system to identify these issues and to begin programs of intervention to address them. This is where The California Endowment's Healthy Returns Initiative begins its work, increasing access to health care services for detained youth.<br><br>The 130,000 youth who leave county and state facilities every year have historically had inadequate support, particularly for health care. But now, because of the Healthy Returns Initiative, many of these young people have improved access to health care after release as well. Healthy Returns is at work in five California counties—Santa Clara, Santa Cruz, Ventura, Humboldt, and Los Angeles—bringing together probation departments, health care providers, schools and families.<br><br>For some counties, this increased emphasis on prevention rather than punishment might present a challenge, but not in these counties. In these counties, probation departments, juvenile court judges, and local civic authorities have all supported the initiative's goal to promote interagency collaboration and think about juvenile justice from a public health perspective. |

## Summary

Despite the challenges of evaluation, there are growing numbers of examples of effective practices in a number of intervention areas. Getting "inside the black box" of effective programs to accumulate knowledge about how and why these programs work is an exciting frontier of current evaluation research.

In sum, the framework outlined in Chapter Two provides a scheme for organizing approaches to improving the odds for boys and men of color. We did not conduct a comprehensive review of these approaches, but rather argue that there are different types of levers that can be used to improve the odds at the macro-, community, and interpersonal and individual levels. Furthermore, there is a large and growing body of research-based information that can help policymakers implement effective strategies for altering the odds faced by these young people. A common theme across all potential levels of intervention is the value of collecting information to provide an accurate understanding of where disparities exist and what levers may best be able to mitigate them.

# Conclusions

*Across the four sets of outcomes summarized in this report, we find that odds for boys and men of color are a lot worse (more than two times worse) than for white boys and men for the following highly disparate indicators:*

- **Socioeconomic.** Both Latino and African-American children are at increased risk for *living in poverty*. Relative to whites, African Americans and Latinos are at increased risk for *low maternal education*. African-American children are more likely than whites to *live in single-parent households* and to *live in households where no parents are employed year-round full-time*.

- **Health.** African Americans in California are at increased odds relative to whites for *infant mortality, very low birth weight, births to unmarried women, births to teen mothers,* and *being hospitalized for asthma*. Latinos in California are at increased risk for *births to unmarried women, births to teen mothers, being overweight, being uninsured,* and *having no usual source of care* when compared with whites. Nationally, both Latinos and African Americans are at increased risk for *HIV/AIDS* and *PTSD*.

- **Safety.** African Americans in California are at increased odds relative to whites for being *incarcerated and disproportionately represented in the prison population, arrested as a juvenile, the victim of substantiated child abuse and neglect, a witness of domestic violence,* and *placed in foster care*. Both African Americans and Latinos are at increased odds for the *lifetime likelihood of going to prison, having an incarcerated parent, being in custody, fire-arms-related deaths,* and

*"... African Americans and Latinos have increased odds relative to whites of being exposed to other forms of violence such as shootings, bombs or riots."*

*homicide-related deaths.* In addition, African Americans and Latinos have increased odds relative to whites of being *exposed to other forms of violence such as shootings, bombs or riots.* For most of these indicators, the magnitude of the increased odds is highest for African-Americans.

- **Ready to Learn.** Relative to whites in California, Latinos are at increased risk for *having less than a high school degree.* In California, both Latino and African-American children are at increased risk for *being below basic proficiency in math and in reading.* African-American students are also more likely than whites to be *suspended from school or retained in grade.*

As the results above indicate, different patterns emerge in the four outcome areas. In the area of *socioeconomic* indicators, we find that both Latino and African-American children are more likely to live in poverty and that African-American children are more likely to live in single-parent families and families where no adults work fulltime year round. In one of the greatest disparities measured in this report, we observed that Latino children are more than ten times more likely to have mothers with less education than a high school degree. African-American children are also at greater risk of having mothers with low education levels, but at a lower rate of two and a half times, rather than more than ten times.

In the *health* area, the indicators for which African Americans had the greatest disparity (three times or more) were births to unmarried women, hospitalization for asthma, and HIV or AIDS. For Latinos, some of the largest disparities were seen in the areas of births to teen mothers, PTSD, HIV or AIDS, and being uninsured. In a few cases, Latinos but not African Americans have relative odds that met the criteria, but for these indicators, African Americans are at least at elevated risk.

Across all the *safety* indicators shown, African Americans' odds are worse than those of Latinos. When both groups were at increased risk, the odds for African Americans were often two or three times worse than the odds for Latinos, indicating the intensity of the disparities for African Americans. Some of the greatest disparities we observed were for African Americans' homicide-related and firearms-related death rates.

Finally, in the *ready to learn* area, the increased odds for Latinos and African Americans are comparable and focused within the achievement and proficiency indicators. African-American students were also at increased risk for being held back a grade and being suspended from school.

Although there are large odds working against boys and men of color, there is a growing body of research that identifies approaches at the macro, community, interpersonal and individual levels that can improve those odds. Interventions at these different levels will reinforce and strengthen each other; having an impact on the odds for these young people is likely to require a portfolio of strategies. In sum, the unequal chances that boys and men of color face are not immutable, and we know an increasing amount about how to improve those chances.

Many of the highly disparate indicators that rose to the surface—for example, poor health behaviors and lack of access to services—are what are known as "modifiable conditions," which can be improved and that, as a result, can lead to better outcomes. Although in theory these conditions are modifiable, it is important to note that they occur in a social and community context with severe structural constraints, which makes it very challenging to address them. With this in mind, one approach to improving the odds for boys and men of color would be to implement interventions that target these conditions. Examples might include programs that improve educational achievement or reduce children's exposure to violence. Another approach to improving the odds for boys and men of color would be to implement interventions that would help improve neighborhood-level conditions.

The relative odds of the identified indicators—how much they are above the two-times worse threshold set here—do not by themselves provide a comprehensive basis for targeting efforts. Other considerations might include whether programs that target the indicators exist, whether there is evidence that existing programs work for boys and men of color, what the relative costs of alternative programs are, how much of an impact improving the indicator will have on society, and what effects improving the indicator will have for the individual or for his expected mortality. Questions such as these might help guide decisions about how to target efforts to improve the odds.

To the extent possible, we drew upon data from California; however, for some indicators only national-level data were available. Likewise, we provide data for boys and men whenever possible. Also, data for Asians and Native Americans were sparse and so we focused this report on African Americans and Latinos. Any programmatic or policy response will require more complete data for boys and men of color.

Within this framework of macro-, community and interpersonal and individual-level factors, national organizations such as the National Urban League, the Joint Center for Political and Economic Studies, the Congressional Hispanic Caucus, and national foundations such as the W.K. Kellogg Foundation and the Ford Foundation have made major contributions to understanding disparities among racial and ethnic groups and to develop an action agenda for addressing these inequalities. The 2006 Dellums Commission report undertook a comprehensive examination of a range of policies that limit the life chances of young men of color and their communities and made a number of recommendations for policy change. Collectively, this body of work has led to important steps at the national level, such as federal legislation to establish an Office of Men's Health within DHHS to examine the social determinants of health.

The California Endowment also has taken a leadership role in addressing the social determinants underlying such disparities that exist in California. This commissioned report is intended to contribute to the statewide conversation on this important set of issues by shedding light on key inequalities within California for boys and men of color.

Identifying disparities is only a starting point. Understanding the underlying causes of racial and ethnic disparities is a critical next step for developing an action agenda for California. This type of examination was beyond the scope of this project; instead, this report is designed to help readers understand some of the basic facts related to the odds for boys and men of color in California. But beyond that, we hope that the report will help identify some starting points in the policy arena for diminishing the disparities for boys and men of color in the state. The disparities in the indicators shown here can be used as a baseline to measure progress in narrowing the gap over time.

"*Understanding* the underlying
causes of racial and ethnic disparities is
*a critical next step* for developing an
action agenda for California."

# Appendix: Summary of Other Outcome Indicators

*In the main report, we provided detailed information on areas where the greatest disparities for boys and men of color exist as a way to identify possible starting points for addressing these disparities.*

We worked with The California Endowment to identify four broad outcome domains—socioeconomic, health, safety, and ready to learn—and to select specific indicators that are most commonly used to characterize each domain from a range of possibilities. While any disproportion in odds is a concern, we focused on those indicators where the odds are *two times greater or more* for boys and men of color relative to their white peers.

In this appendix, we present the results for indicators that did not meet the "two times greater or more" threshold. In addition, there were a few indicators that did meet this threshold yet were similar to those presented in the main report; for example, we presented one indicator for sexually transmitted disease (HIV or AIDS) in the main report and present the remaining sexually transmitted disease indicators here in the appendix. This appendix summarizes the findings for all indicators not covered in the main document for each of the four domains.

## Socioeconomic

In the socioeconomic context outcome area, we examined the indicators shown in the scorecard (see **Table A.1**). This table and the other scorecard tables show the indicators, the odds ratios for Latino and African-American boys and men of color relative to their white counterparts, and information about the data. As shown, the relative odds for boys and men of color for all these indicators exceeded the 2.0 threshold for either Latinos or African Americans or both, except for one—youth unemployment—which we discuss here; the remaining indicators are discussed in the summary report.

## TABLE A.1

### Odds Relative to Whites by Race/Ethnicity for Socioeconomic Indicators.

| Indicator | Latino | African-American | Relev. Geo Area | Gender | Year |
|---|---|---|---|---|---|
| Children living in poverty | 3.4 | 3.4 | CA | Both | 2005 |
| Maternal education (less than high school) | 10.2 | 2.0 | CA | Both | 2005 |
| Children living in single-parent households | 1.1 | 2.5 | CA | Both | 2005 |
| Children with unemployed parents | 1.6 | 2.4 | US | Both | 2005 |
| Youth unemployment | 1.2 | 1.6 | CA | Both | 2004 |

### Youth Unemployment

Unemployment rates by race and ethnicity among young people in California generally mirror those found in the rest of the country (see **Figure A.1**). Young men tend to experience higher unemployment rates than young women, and African Americans have the highest rates followed by Latinos.

## Health

In the health outcome area, we examined the indicators shown in the scorecard (see **Table A.2**). Information on the indicators that have odds less than 2.0 are discussed below, while the indicators with odds of 2.0 or more are discussed in the body of the report.

### Childhood Asthma

In the summary report, we discuss the one indicator for asthma that is above the 2.0 threshold—hospitalization for asthma. Here, we discuss the other asthma indicators we examined that did not meet the 2.0 threshold.

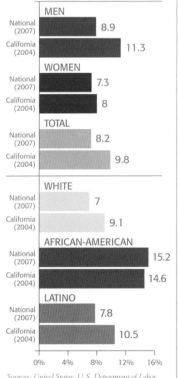

## FIGURE A.1

### Unemployment Rate for 20-24 year olds, by gender and race/Hispanic origin (percent).

Sources: United States: U.S. Department of Labor, Bureau of Labor Statistics, 2008. California: U.S. Department of Labor, Bureau of Labor Statistics, 2004.

TABLE
A.2

# Odds Relative to Whites by Race/Ethnicity for Health Indicators.

| Indicator | Latino | African-American | Relev. Geo Area | Gender | Year |
|---|---|---|---|---|---|
| Low birth weight* | 0.95 | 1.9 | CA | Both | 2005 |
| Very low birth weight | 1.0 | 2.6 | CA | Both | 2005 |
| Births to unmarried women | 2.2 | 3.0 | CA | Female | 2005 |
| Births to teen mothers | 3.6 | 2.2 | CA | Female | 2003 |
| Infant mortality | 1.2 | 2.8 | CA | Male | 2004 |
| **Childhood Asthma** | | | | | |
| • Active asthma | 0.7 | 1.7 | CA | Both | 2003 |
| • ER visits for asthma | 1.4 | 1.7 | CA | Both | 2003 |
| • Hospitalization for asthma | 1.1 | 3.7 | CA | Male | 2005 |
| • School absence due to asthma | 1.5 | 1.4 | CA | Both | 2003 |
| Childhood obesity | 2.0 | 0.8* | CA | Male | 2005 |
| **Social/Emotional Well-Being** | | | | | |
| • Depression | 1.1 | 1.1 | CA | Both | 2005 |
| • Felt sad | 1.0 | 0.9 | CA | Both | 2005 |
| • PTSD | 4.1 | 2.5 | US | Both | 1995 |
| **Alcohol/Substance Use** | | | | | |
| • Recent alcohol use | 0.8 | 0.6 | CA | Male | 2005 |
| • Binge drinking | 0.7 | 0.3 | CA | Male | 2005 |
| • Cocaine use | 1.6 | 0.3 | US | Both | 2005 |
| • Heroin use | 1.6 | 0.7 | US | Both | 2005 |
| • SA/dependence | – | 0.3 | US | Both | 2005 |
| • Smoking | 0.6 | 0.5 | CA | Both | 2003 |
| **Sexually Transmitted Diseases** | | | | | |
| • HIV and AIDS | 3.1 | 6.9 | US | Male | 2005 |
| • Chlamydia | 2.3 | 7.3 | CA | Male | 2006 |
| • Gonorrhea | 1.7 | 12.7 | CA | Male | 2006 |
| • Syphilis | 1.7 | 4.2 | CA | Male | 2006 |
| Health Insurance (lack of) | 4.8 | 0.6* | CA | Male | 2005 |
| **Limited to Health Care** | | | | | |
| • No usual source of care (0-11 years) | 2.5 | 1.1 | CA | Male | 2005 |
| • No usual source of care (12-17 years) | 2.0 | 1.7 | CA | Both | 2005 |
| • ED room visits (0-11 yrs) | 0.9 | 1.6 | CA | Both | 2003 |
| • ED room visits (12-17 yrs) | 0.8 | 1.2 | CA | Both | 2003 |

Note, Low birth weight is discussed in the body of the report (See Chapter Three) in conjunction with the discussion on very low birth weight.
*Estimates are unreliable due to small cell sizes.

Nationally, African-American children are 1.3 times more likely than white children to have been told that they have asthma (Bloom and Cohen, 2007). In California, the prevalence of active asthma in African-American children is 1.7 times that of white children (see **Figure A.2**).

For children with asthma, access to timely health care is important to effectively manage the condition (Meng et al., 2007). In California, African-American children (ages 0 to 17) with asthma were 2.6 times more likely to not have a usual place of care than white children with asthma.[16] Latino children (ages 0 to 17) with asthma were more than twice as likely as white children to not have health insurance either part of or the entire previous year.[17]

Disproportionality in asthma burden among California children can be measured also by emergency department visits for asthma (Meng et al., 2007). In 2003, African-American children were disproportionately affected by asthma exacerbations that resulted in emergency department visits. Of those with asthma, 33 percent of African-American children and 26 percent of Latino children had at least one emergency department visit for an asthma exacerbation, compared with 19 percent of white children (see **Figure A.3**).

Asthma is also a factor related to school absenteeism among children with active asthma, especially Latinos. Among children with active asthma, Latino children were nearly twice as likely as white children to have missed at least one day of school during the past 12 months (see **Figure A.4**).

### Social and Emotional Well-Being

In the summary report, we discuss post-traumatic stress disorder (PTSD), which met the 2.0 threshold. Here, we discuss the other social and emotional well-being indicators that did not meet that threshold.

[16] *Of African-American children with asthma, 16.4 percent (S.E. 4.73) indicated they did not have a usual place of care compared with 6.4 percent (S.E. 1.74) of white children. Estimates for Latino, American Indian, and Asian children were statistically unstable (California Health Interview Survey, 2007a).*

[17] *Of Latino children (ages 0–17) with asthma, 10.9 percent (S.E. 2.6) had no insurance the entire or part of the previous year as compared with 4.7 percent (S.E. 1.19) of white children. Estimates for African-American, Native American and Asian children were statistically unstable (California Health Interview Survey, 2007a).*

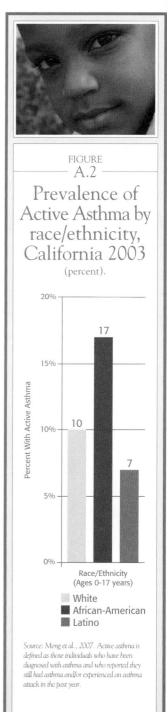

FIGURE
A.2

Prevalence of Active Asthma by race/ethnicity, California 2003
(percent).

Percent With Active Asthma

White: 10
African-American: 17
Latino: 7

Race/Ethnicity
(Ages 0-17 years)

■ White
■ African-American
■ Latino

*Source: Meng et al., 2007. Active asthma is defined as those individuals who have been diagnosed with asthma and who reported they still had asthma and/or experienced an asthma attack in the past year.*

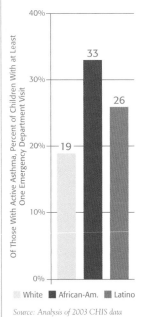

FIGURE
A.3

Percent of children (age 0-17) with at least one Emergency Department visit for Asthma by race/ethnicity among those with active Asthma, California 2003.

Of Those With Active Asthma, Percent of Children With at Least One Emergency Department Visit

40%

30%

33

30%

26

20%

19

10%

0%

White    African-Am.    Latino

Source: Analysis of 2003 CHIS data (California Health Interview Survey).

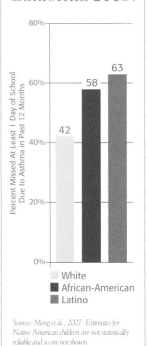

FIGURE
A.4

Percent of children (age 5-11) who missed at least 1 day of school due to Asthma among those with active Asthma, California 2003.

80%

Percent Missed At Least 1 Day of School Due to Asthma in Past 12 Months

60%

63

58

42

40%

20%

0%

White
African-American
Latino

Source: Meng et al., 2007. Estimates for Native American children are not statistically reliable and so are not shown.

In adolescence, social and emotional health becomes increasingly important in the developmental process. Depression is a mental condition that can affect all aspects of a person's life. Some of the symptoms of depression include losing interest in things, feeling persistently sad or anxious, having no energy and being unable to sleep normally. Depression in adolescents is often difficult to diagnose, since adolescence is a time of increasing social and emotional change (U.S. Department of Health and Human Services, 1999). When an adolescent becomes depressed, then he is at risk for a variety of poor outcomes. For example, depressed adolescents are more likely to have problems with school performance, peer and family relationships, and substance abuse, and are more likely to engage in risky sexual behavior. Persistent and severe depression can lead to a more confined life with few friends and supports and ultimately to suicide. Some of the risk factors for depression among adolescents include chronic illness, family history of depression, child abuse, stressful life events, anxiety and smoking (Bhatia and Bhatia, 2007).

In California, 38 percent of adolescents ages 12 to 17 reported feeling depressed in the last week, and 49 percent reported feeling sad during that time (see **Figure A.5**). While slightly higher percentages of Latino (41 percent) and African-American (41 percent) adolescents ages 12 to 17 reported feeling depressed in the past seven days when compared with white (38 percent) and Asian adolescents (35 percent), the differences were not statistically significant. The percentages of those reporting that they had felt sad in the past seven days were also similar across different racial and ethnic groups, with 47 percent of African-American adolescents and 52 percent of Latino and white adolescents indicating that they had felt sad within the last week. Looking at adolescent boys, about one-third of African-American, Latino and white boys reported feeling depressed in the past seven days and around 40 percent reported feeling sad in the past seven days.[B]

### Alcohol and Substance Use

As shown in **Table A.2**, none of the alcohol and substance use indicators reached the 2.0 threshold. Thus, we discuss them here. Alcohol and substance use often lead to social, emotional, and behavioral problems that carry immediate risk and that may also persevere into adulthood. Adolescents who use alcohol or drugs are at increased risk for engaging in criminal activity and risky sexual behavior, depression, poor school performance, impaired driving, and alcohol or substance dependence in adulthood (Komro and Toomey, 2002). Some of the risk factors for adolescent alcohol and substance use include behavior problems, psychiatric disorders, suicidal behavior, parental drinking, lack of parental support and communication, peer drinking, child abuse and other trauma (National Institute on Alcohol Abuse and Alcoholism, 1997).

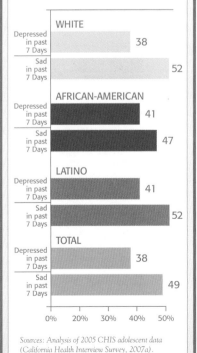

FIGURE
A.5

Percent of adolescents (age 12-17) in California in 2005 who ever felt depressed in past 7 days and who ever felt sad in past 7 days, by race/ethnicity.

**WHITE**
Depressed in past 7 Days: 38
Sad in past 7 Days: 52

**AFRICAN-AMERICAN**
Depressed in past 7 Days: 41
Sad in past 7 Days: 47

**LATINO**
Depressed in past 7 Days: 41
Sad in past 7 Days: 52

**TOTAL**
Depressed in past 7 Days: 38
Sad in past 7 Days: 49

0%   20%   30%   40%   50%

Sources: Analysis of 2005 CHIS adolescent data (California Health Interview Survey, 2007a).

[B] *While females report depressive symptoms more often than their male counterparts, the percentages of California female adolescents who felt depressed or sad in the past week do not differ substantially by race and ethnicity.*

FIGURE
A.6

Percent of 12-20 year-olds who drank in the past 30 days, by gender and race/Hispanic origin.

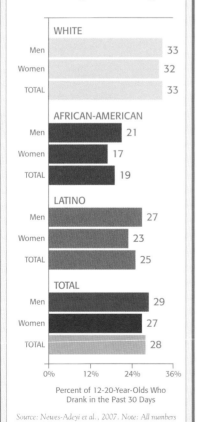

WHITE
- Men — 33
- Women — 32
- TOTAL — 33

AFRICAN-AMERICAN
- Men — 21
- Women — 17
- TOTAL — 19

LATINO
- Men — 27
- Women — 23
- TOTAL — 25

TOTAL
- Men — 29
- Women — 27
- TOTAL — 28

Percent of 12-20-Year-Olds Who Drank in the Past 30 Days

Source: Newes-Adeyi et al., 2007. Note: All numbers are rounded.

Nationally, more than one quarter (28 percent) of 12–20 year-olds reported drinking within the last 30 days in 2005 (see **Figure A.6**). Similar percentages of males and females reported drinking within the last month. Looking across different racial and ethnic groups, a larger percentage of whites (33 percent) and Latinos (25 percent) reported drinking within the past 30 days than African Americans (19 percent). White males were 1.5 times more likely than African-American males to have drunk in the last 30 days. Latino males were 1.3 times more likely than African-American men to report recent drinking.

Since 1991 the percentage of adolescents and young adults who reported drinking in the last 30 days has declined by 15 percent (Newes-Adeyi et al., 2007). While all racial and ethnic groups experienced declines in drinking behavior, there were differences by race and ethnicity. The prevalence decreased by only 7 percent for non-Hispanic whites. The percentage for Hispanic 12–20 year-olds decreased 19 percent, while the percent decrease for non-Hispanic African Americans was 36 percent.

In California, more than one-third of adolescents 12 to 17 reported ever having more than a few sips of alcohol in the past month (see **Figure A.7**). Similar to the national data, white adolescents reported more drinking (41 percent) than either Latino (34 percent) or African-American adolescents (26 percent). White males were 1.6 times more likely than African-American males and 1.2 times more likely than Latino males to report drinking in the last month. Among females, white females were 1.1 times more likely than African-American females to report recent drinking.

It is also important to look at more serious binge drinking when examining the impact of adolescent risk behavior on healthy development. Binge drinking is defined as having five or more drinks in a row in a short time period. Nationally, nearly one-fifth (19 percent) of 12–20-year-olds reported binge drinking in the past 30 days (see **Figure A.8**). As with any drinking, whites (22 percent) and Latinos (17 percent) reported binge drinking more often than African Americans (9 percent). For this age group, males reported binge drinking more often than females, both overall and across different racial and ethnic groups. White adolescents and young men were more than two times as likely to report binge drinking as African Americans. Latinos were at 1.7 times greater risk of binge drinking when compared with African Americans.

In California, the pattern of binge drinking by gender and race looks a little different. Overall, 7 percent of adolescents 12 to 17 reported binge drinking in the past month (see **Figure A.9**). Latinos and whites were all more likely to report binge drinking than African Americans. White males were 3.6 times more likely to report binge drinking than African-American males. Latino adolescents were at 1.4 times greater risk of binge drinking when compared with African-American adolescents.

FIGURE
A.7

Percent of adolescents 12-17 in California who ever had more than a few sips of alcohol in the past month, by gender and race/Hispanic origin.

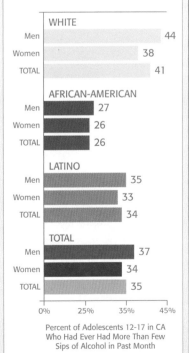

WHITE
Men — 44
Women — 38
TOTAL — 41

AFRICAN-AMERICAN
Men — 27
Women — 26
TOTAL — 26

LATINO
Men — 35
Women — 33
TOTAL — 34

TOTAL
Men — 37
Women — 34
TOTAL — 35

0%    25%    35%    45%

Percent of Adolescents 12-17 in CA
Who Had Ever Had More Than Few
Sips of Alcohol in Past Month

*Source: Analysis of 2005 CHIS adolescent data
(California Health Interview Survey, 2007a).
Note: All numbers are rounded.*

FIGURE
A.8

Percent of 12-20 year-olds who reported *binge* drinking in the past 30 days, by gender and race/Hispanic origin.

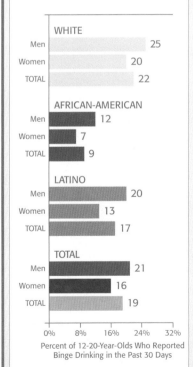

WHITE
Men — 25
Women — 20
TOTAL — 22

AFRICAN-AMERICAN
Men — 12
Women — 7
TOTAL — 9

LATINO
Men — 20
Women — 13
TOTAL — 17

TOTAL
Men — 21
Women — 16
TOTAL — 19

0%    8%    16%    24%    32%

Percent of 12-20-Year-Olds Who Reported
Binge Drinking in the Past 30 Days

*Source: Newes-Adeyi et al., 2007.
Note: All numbers are rounded.*

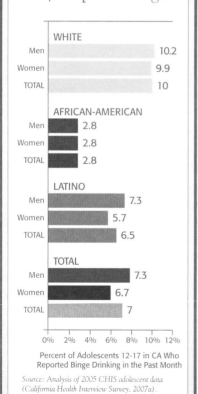

FIGURE
A.9

Percent of adolescents 12-17 in California who reported *binge* drinking in the past month, by race/Hispanic origin.

**WHITE**

| | |
|---|---|
| Men | 10.2 |
| Women | 9.9 |
| TOTAL | 10 |

**AFRICAN-AMERICAN**

| | |
|---|---|
| Men | 2.8 |
| Women | 2.8 |
| TOTAL | 2.8 |

**LATINO**

| | |
|---|---|
| Men | 7.3 |
| Women | 5.7 |
| TOTAL | 6.5 |

**TOTAL**

| | |
|---|---|
| Men | 7.3 |
| Women | 6.7 |
| TOTAL | 7 |

0%  2%  4%  6%  8%  10%  12%

Percent of Adolescents 12-17 in CA Who Reported Binge Drinking in the Past Month

Source: Analysis of 2005 CHIS adolescent data (California Health Interview Survey, 2007a).

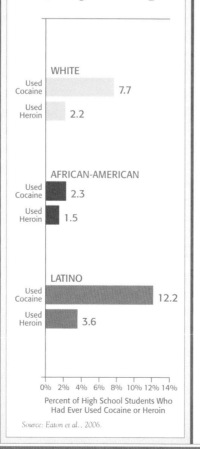

FIGURE
A.10

Percent of high school students who had ever used cocaine or ever used heroin, by race/Hispanic origin.

**WHITE**

| | |
|---|---|
| Used Cocaine | 7.7 |
| Used Heroin | 2.2 |

**AFRICAN-AMERICAN**

| | |
|---|---|
| Used Cocaine | 2.3 |
| Used Heroin | 1.5 |

**LATINO**

| | |
|---|---|
| Used Cocaine | 12.2 |
| Used Heroin | 3.6 |

0%  2%  4%  6%  8%  10%  12%  14%

Percent of High School Students Who Had Ever Used Cocaine or Heroin

Source: Eaton et al., 2006.

For substance use, we focused on cocaine and heroin, since those were the most prevalent type of drugs with disparities. Nationally, in 2005 Latino students were more likely than African-American and white students to have ever used cocaine or heroin (see **Figure A.10**). African-American students were less likely than Latino and white students to have ever used cocaine. When compared with white high school students, Latinos were 1.6 times more likely to have used cocaine in their lifetime and 1.6 times as likely to have ever used heroin. Latino high school students were 5.3 times more likely than African-American students to have ever used cocaine and 2.4 times more likely to have ever used heroin. Data were not available by race and ethnicity for California.

More serious substance use can rise to the level of an officially diagnosed mental disorder. In a national probability sample of adolescents 12 to 17 years of age, the 12-month substance abuse/dependency prevalence was 8.2 percent for males and 6.3 percent for females. The odds of an African-American adolescent having diagnosed substance abuse/dependence were one-third that of a white adolescent (Kilpatrick et al., 2003).

Like other risky health behaviors, cigarette smoking often starts in adolescence. Adolescents who smoke are at increased risk for a variety of poor outcomes. In terms of their health, adolescents who smoke are more likely to have respiratory problems, be physically unfit, and develop chronic conditions in adulthood. Smoking is also related to a variety of risky behaviors. An adolescent who smokes has increased odds for drinking, using drugs, engaging in unprotected sex and carrying weapons. The risk factors for the development of adolescent smoking include poverty, single-parent homes and peer influence (U.S. Department of Health and Human Services, 1994).

Nationally, in 2005 nearly one-quarter (23 percent) of high school students currently smoked cigarettes (Eaton et al., 2006). The percentages varied by race and ethnicity with white high school students (26%) reporting more smoking than Latino (22 percent) or African-American (13 percent) high school students. Overall, white high school students were 3 times more likely to currently smoke than African-American high school students. Latino students were at 1.8 times greater risk for smoking when compared with African-American students.

In California, the percentage of adolescents 12 to 17 who reported currently smoked was highest among whites (see **Figure A.11**). White adolescents were at 2.1 times greater risk of smoking than African-American adolescents and 1.7 times greater risk than Latino adolescents. White adolescent males were 2.2 times more likely than African-American males to report current smoking.

## Access to Health Care

As shown in **Table A.2**, usual source of care rises above the threshold and is discussed in the summary report. However, another indicator of access to care is use of emergency room visits, which, as shown in the table, does not rise above the threshold and is discussed here. This indicator can reflect a number of things including use of the ER for urgent care, as a substitute for usual source of care, and/or a source of care for unmet medical needs.

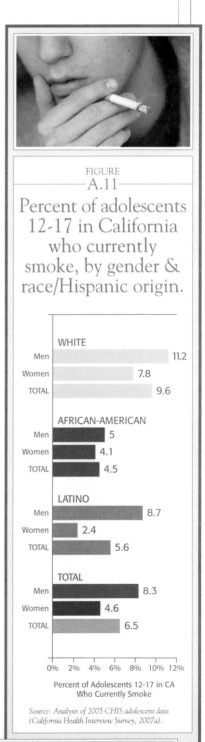

FIGURE
A.11

Percent of adolescents 12-17 in California who currently smoke, by gender & race/Hispanic origin.

WHITE
Men 11.2
Women 7.8
TOTAL 9.6

AFRICAN-AMERICAN
Men 5
Women 4.1
TOTAL 4.5

LATINO
Men 8.7
Women 2.4
TOTAL 5.6

TOTAL
Men 8.3
Women 4.6
TOTAL 6.5

Percent of Adolescents 12-17 in CA Who Currently Smoke

*Source: Analysis of 2005 CHIS adolescent data (California Health Interview Survey, 2007a).*

FIGURE
A.12

Emergency room
visits in the past 12
months, children
and adolescents,
California 2003.

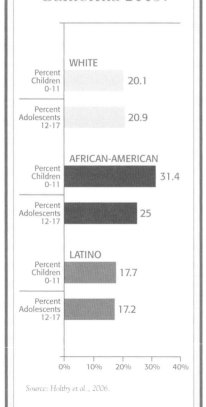

WHITE

Percent Children 0-11 — 20.1

Percent Adolescents 12-17 — 20.9

AFRICAN-AMERICAN

Percent Children 0-11 — 31.4

Percent Adolescents 12-17 — 25

LATINO

Percent Children 0-11 — 17.7

Percent Adolescents 12-17 — 17.2

0%   10%   20%   30%   40%

*Source: Holtby et al., 2006.*

Nationally, based on results from the 2006 National Health Interview Survey, use of the ER by children varied by race and ethnicity, single-parent and two-parent families, and source of coverage (Centers for Disease Control and Prevention 2008).

- Non-Hispanic African American children were more likely to have had two or more visits to an emergency room in the past 12 months (10 percent) than non-Hispanic white children (7 percent) or Hispanic children (7 percent).

- Children in single-mother families were more likely to have had two or more visits to an emergency room in the past 12 months (11 percent) compared with children in two-parent families (7 percent).

- Children with Medicaid or other public coverage were more likely to have had two or more emergency room visits in the past 12 months (10 percent) than children with no health insurance (7 percent) or children with private health insurance (6 percent).

Analysis of the 2003 California Health Interview Survey (CHIS) data found that, similar to the national picture, African-American children (0 to 11 years) were more likely than white children to have had an emergency room visit in the past year (see **Figure A.12**). Among adolescents, there was no statistically significant difference in the percentage of African-American, Latino or white adolescents on this measure. However, Asian children and adolescents were less likely than white children to have had any emergency room visits during this time period.

## Sexually Transmitted Diseases

Although Chlamydia, Gonorrhea and Syphilis met the 2.0 criterion, for brevity's sake The California Endowment requested that the report focus primarily on HIV and AIDS odds. We present here the data for these other sexually transmitted diseases (STDs). In California, there are stark differences in the rates of STDs for young men of color (see **Table A.2**). For Chlamydia, African-American males ages 20 to 24 have a 7.3 times greater risk of Chlamydia than white males of the same age. Latino males are 2.3 times more likely to contract Chlamydia. For Gonorrhea, African-American males between the ages of 20 and 24 are 12.7 times more likely and Latino males are 1.7 times more likely than white males to contract Gonorrhea. For Syphilis, African-American males ages 20 to 24 are 4.2 times as likely and Latino males are 1.7 times as likely to have Syphilis.

STDs like Chlamydia, Gonorrhea and Syphilis cause serious health problems. Syphilis manifests as sores and can lead to rashes and lesions and eventually to damage to the internal organs in the late stage. All three of these STDs are spread through vaginal, anal and oral sex and are believed to facilitate the spread of HIV (Steele et al, 2005), another serious health problem.

## Safety

In the safety outcome area, we examined the indicators shown in the scorecard **Table A.4**. Information on the indicators that have odds were less than 2.0 are shown below, while those above the 2.0 threshold are discussed in the summary

TABLE
A.3

### Sexually Transmitted Disease Rates.
*(per 100,000 adult males ages 20-24)*

| Race/Ethnicity | Chlamydia | Gonorrhea | Syphilis |
|---|---|---|---|
| White | 338 | 110 | 7.6 |
| African-American | 2472 | 1397 | 31.9 |
| Latino | 769 | 185 | 12.9 |

*Source: California Department of Public Health, 2007a.*

report. There are several exceptions: fatal domestic violence rates and some indicators of witnessing violence/indirect victimization. For brevity's sake, The California Endowment requested that we present these indicators in the appendix rather than in the summary report, even though they met the 2.0 threshold.

TABLE
A.4

# Odds Relative to Whites by Race/Ethnicity for Safety Indicators.

| Indicator | Latino | African-American | Relev. Geo Area | Gender | Year |
|---|---|---|---|---|---|
| Lifetime likelihood of ever going to prison | 2.9 | 5.5 | US | Male | 2001 |
| Disproportional representation in prison population* | 1.07 | 4.33 | CA | Male | 2007 |
| Incarceration rate | 1.5 | 6.7 | CA | Male | 2005 |
| Children with incarcerated parents | 3.3 | 8.8 | US | Both | 1999 |
| **Three Strikes Conviction** | | | | | |
| • Total striker population | 1.4 | 1.4 | CA | Male | 2007 |
| • Third striker population | 1.0 | 1.8 | CA | Male | 2007 |
| Juvenile arrest rate | 1.2 | 2.5 | CA | Both | 2005 |
| Juvenile custody rate | 2.1 | 5.7 | CA | Male | 2003 |
| Firearms-related death rate | 3.3 | 10.1 | CA | Male | 2004 |
| Homicide-related death rate | 5.1 | 16.4 | CA | Male | 2004 |
| **Domestic Violence** | | | | | |
| • Fatal domestic violence rates | 1.6 | 4.4 | CA | Both | 01-05 |
| • Non-fatal domestic violence rates | 0.8 | 1.8 | US | Male | 1987-00 |
| **Exposure to Other Forms of Violence** | | | | | |
| • Property crime victimization | – | 1.4 | US | Both | 2006 |
| • Violent crime victimization | – | 1.2 | US | Both | 2006 |
| • Witnessing/indirect victimization | | | US | Both | 02/03 |
|   – Witnessing domestic violence | 1.1 | 2.1 | US | Both | 02/03 |
|   – Exposure to shootings, bombs, riots | 2.1 | 3.0 | US | Both | 02/03 |
|   – Any witnessing and indirect victimization | 1.1 | 1.3 | US | Both | 02/03 |
| Substantiated child abuse and neglect | 1.3 | 2.5 | CA | Both | 2005 |
| Foster care* | .89 | 4.05 | CA | Both | 2004 |

* This is not an odds ratio, but rather it is a disproportionality index number. For foster care, the index represents the proportion of children in the foster care system when compared with that group's overall proportion in the general population. An index number below 1.00 indicates an underrepresentation in foster care compared with the proportion in the general child population, while a number above 1.00 indicates an overrepresentation of children in foster care. For the prison population, the index represents the proportion of African-Americans or Latinos in the prison population compared with each group's overall proportion in the general population. An index number above 1.00 indicates an overrepresentation in the prison population.

## Three Strikes Conviction

In 1994, California's Three Strikes law was enacted requiring a minimum sentence of 25 years to life for three-time repeat offenders with multiple prior serious or violent felony convictions. The Three Strikes legislation was in response to concerns that violent offenders were being released from prison and back into the community, where they were committing new, often serious and violent, crimes.

California is the only state where any felony offense can trigger a Three Strikes sentence.[18] California "strikes out" four times as many individuals as other Three-Strikes states combined.[19] Since its enactment, Three Strikes has had a major impact on the growth and composition of the prison population.

The courts have sent more than 80,000 second strikers and 7,500 third strikers to California state prison since 1994 (Schiraldi, Colburn, and Lotke, 2004). As of the end of December 2004, almost 43,000 inmates were serving time in prison under the Three Strikes law (26 percent of total prison population). Of the striker population, more than 35,000 are second strikers and 7,500 are third strikers.

In terms of the racial composition of strikers, African-American males are disproportionately represented among the second and third striker population. African-American males (45 percent) comprise the largest group of second and third strikers, followed by Latino males (26 percent) and white males (25 percent) (see **Table A.5**).

## Witnessing Domestic Violence

Domestic violence, or intimate partner violence, is violence committed by someone known to the victim such as a current or former spouse or partner. For the victim, intimate partner violence can lead to physical injury and health problems, emotional problems, trauma symptoms, alcohol or substance

[18] A felony conviction need not be serious or violent (Schiraldi, Colburn, and Lotke, 2004).
[19] Expressed as a rate per 100,000 residents, California's Three Strikes rate (119.3) is 18 times as great as the average for the other Three Strikes states (Schiraldi, Colburn, and Lotke, 2004).

abuse and sometimes death (National Center for Injury Prevention and Control, 2003). Children often witness domestic violence and their exposure to violence can have consequences for their development. Children exposed to violence are more likely to have internalizing and externalizing behavior problems (Peled, Jaffe, and Endleson, 1995). Children who witness violence are at increased risk for becoming victims themselves, suffering from PTSD, abusing alcohol or drugs, running away from home and engaging in criminal activity (Family Violence Prevention Fund, 2002).

TABLE
A.5

## Second and Third Strikers Males in the Adult Institution Population by Race/Ethnicity, as of December 31, 2007

| Race/Ethnicity | 2nd Strike Pop. Number (Percent) | 3rd Strike Pop. Number (Percent) | Total Striker Pop. Number (Percent) |
|---|---|---|---|
| White | 8,115 (25.14) | 2,065 (25.23) | 10,180 (25.16) |
| African-American | 10,944 (33.90) | 3,658 (44.69) | 14,602 (36.09) |
| Latino | 11,731 (36.35) | 2,119 (25.89) | 13,850 (34.23) |
| Other | 1,485 (4.60) | 344 (4.20) | 1,829 (4.52) |
| Total | 32,275 (100.0) | 8,186 (100.0) | 40,461 (100.0) |

Source: CDCR, 2008a.

Nationally, the average annual rate of nonfatal intimate partner victimization per 1,000 persons age 12 or older was highest among Native Americans of both genders. Since 1993, the rate of nonfatal intimate partner victimization has declined for white, African American and Hispanic females and white males (Catalano, 2007b). Across all racial and ethnic groups, females are victims of domestic violence much more often than men (see **Figure A.13**).

Although intimate partner homicide victimization met the 2.0 criteria, the results for this indicator is reported in this appendix. In California, the rate of intimate partner homicide victimization per 100,000 adults was 4.4 times higher for African-American adults when compared with white adults (see **Figure A.14**). African-American adults were at 2.8 times greater risk than Latino adults of being victims of intimate partner homicide.

### Exposure to Other Forms of Violence

In California, the overall violent crime rate in 2006 was 532.5 per 100,000 population (higher than the U.S. national average of 473.5 violent crimes per 100,000 persons).[20] In both the United States and California, violent crime[21] rates decreased between 1994 and 2004, but then increased in 2005 and 2006. Nationally, violent crimes in the United States fell steadily from 731.8 per 100,000 population in 1994 to 463.2 in 2004; then, they rose between 2005 and 2006 from 469.2 to 473.5. In California, violent crime rates decreased from 1,119.7 per 100,000 population in 1992 to 526.3 in 2005, before rising slightly to 532.5 in 2006 (U.S. Department of Justice, Bureau of Justice Statistics, 2008).

Nationally, males, African-Americans, and individuals 24 years or younger were victimized at higher rates than females, whites, and those 25 years or older in 2005. The overall rate of violence was higher for African Americans (27.0 per 1,000) as compared with whites (20.1 per 1,000); African Americans were also victims of rape, robbery and aggravated assault at higher rates than whites (Catalano, 2006).

[20]  U.S. Department of Justice, Bureau of Justice Statistics data.
[21]  Violent crimes include murder/manslaughter, rape, robberies, and aggravated assaults. The violent crime rate is the number of reported offenses per 100,000 population.

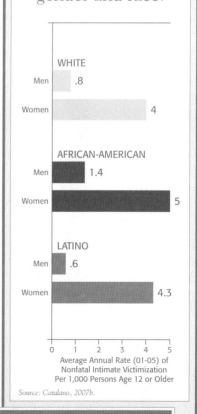

FIGURE
A.13

Average annual rate (2001-2005) of nonfatal intimate partner victimization per 1,000 persons age 12 or older, by gender and race.

WHITE
Men .8
Women 4

AFRICAN-AMERICAN
Men 1.4
Women 5

LATINO
Men .6
Women 4.3

0  1  2  3  4  5
Average Annual Rate (01-05) of Nonfatal Intimate Victimization Per 1,000 Persons Age 12 or Older

Source: Catalano, 2007b.

Overall, African-Americans experienced higher rates of violent crime than did whites (see **Table A.6**). Households headed by African-American individuals also were at greater risk of property victimization than those headed by whites (Catalano, 2007a).

### Witnessing Violence/Indirect Victimization

As shown in **Table A.4** on page 108, when it comes to witnessing violence and indirect victimization, the overall rates do not rise above the threshold. However, a number of more specific rates within the larger category do, including witnessing domestic violence and witnessing a shooting, bombing or riot, which are discussed in the summary report. A few other indicators also rise above the threshold, but in the interest of brevity, The California Endowment asked us to discuss them here, along with the indicators that do not rise above the threshold.

Nationally, African-American children and youth have significantly higher odds of witnessing violence or being victimized indirectly when compared with white children and youth (see **Table A.7**). In terms of the specific types of victimization, the odds of a child or youth witnessing homicide are 20 times

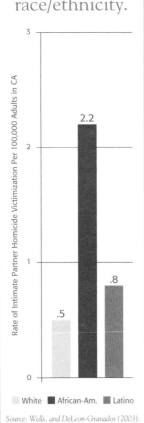

FIGURE
A.14

Rate of intimate partner homicide victimization per 100,000 adults in California, by race/ethnicity.

Source: Wells, and DeLeon-Granados (2003).

TABLE
A.6

## Violent and Property Victimization by Race of Victim or Race of Head of Household, 2006

| Race/Ethnicity | Violent Crime Rate (per 1,000 persons age 12 or older) | Property Crime Rate (per 1,000 households) |
|---|---|---|
| White | 23.2 | 155.80 |
| African-American | 32.7 | 183.6 |

Source: Catalano, 2007a.

higher for African Americans. Latino children and youth have the highest exposure to war. They are 17 times more likely to have been to war than their white counterparts.

Children's exposure to violence can have consequences for their normal development. Children exposed to violence are more likely to have internalizing and externalizing behavior problems (Peled, Jaffe, and Edleson, 1995). Children who witness violence are at increased risk for becoming victims themselves, suffering from PTSD, abusing alcohol or drugs, running away from home and engaging in criminal activity (Family Violence Prevention Fund, 2002).

The Developmental Victimization Survey (DVS), conducted in 2002 and 2003, was designed to fill an information void related to children's exposure to violence (Finkelhor et al., 2005).[22] The survey's objective was to obtain

TABLE
A.7
## Rate of Witnessing or Indirect Victimization.
(per 1,000 Children)

|  | Race or Ethnicity (Rate/1,000 Children) | | |
|---|---|---|---|
|  | White | African-Am. | Latino |
| Any witness or indirect victimization | 335 | 420 | 383 |
| Witness physical abuse | 13 | 7 | 11 |
| Witness assault with weapon | 131 | 160 | 159 |
| Witness assault no weapon | 210 | 250 | 154 |
| Witness murder | 1 | 20 | 0 |
| Exposure to war | 1 | 0 | 17 |
| Someone close murdered | 9 | 70 | 67 |
| Household theft | 85 | 134 | 140 |

Source: Finkelhor et al., 2005.

[22] Estimates of children's and youth's exposure to weapon-related and physical/crime-related community violence have varied widely. Further, the types of victimization that studies have examined differ considerably making it difficult to estimate the burden on children and adolescents (Finkelhor et al., 2008).

FIGURE
A.15

Percent of 8th grade students who were absent from school three or more days in the preceding month, by race and Hispanic origin.

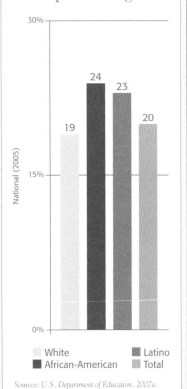

National (2005)

- 30%
- 24
- 23
- 20
- 19
- 15%
- 0%

White
African-American
Latino
Total

Sources: U.S. Department of Education, 2007a.

one-year incidence estimates of a comprehensive range of childhood victimizations across gender, race and developmental stage. A nationally representative sample of 2,030 children ages 2 to 17 years living in the United States was surveyed.

## Ready to Learn

The scorecard (see **Table A.8**) shows the indicators we examined in the ready to learn area. Those that exceeded odds of 2.0 for boys and men of color are discussed in the summary report; here, we report data on the two indicators with odds below 2.0.

### Absenteeism

Absenteeism clearly reduces children's opportunities for learning. White students have the lowest levels of absenteeism (see **Figure A.15**), with Latino students being about 1.2 times more likely to be absent and African-American

TABLE
A.8

### Odds Relative to Whites by Race/Ethnicity for Ready to Learn Indicators.

| Indicator | Latino | African-American | Relev. Geo Area | Gender | Year |
|---|---|---|---|---|---|
| Percent of people over age 25 having less than a high school degree | 6.7 | 1.9 | CA | Both | 2007 |
| Below basic proficiency in reading (grade 4) | 2.3 | 2.2 | CA | Both | 2007 |
| Below basic proficiency in reading (grade 8) | 2.3 | 2.4 | CA | Both | 2007 |
| Below basic proficiency in math (grade 4) | 3.6 | 3.5 | CA | Both | 2007 |
| Below basic proficiency in math (grade 8) | 2.5 | 2.8 | CA | Both | 2007 |
| Absenteeism | 1.2 | 1.3 | US | Both | 2005 |
| School Suspension | 1.2 | 2.4 | US | Male | 2000 |
| Grade Retention | 1.1 | 2.0 | US | Both | 2004 |
| Non-Enrollment in preschool or Pre-K | 1.4 | 0.9 | CA | Both | 2001 |

students about 1.3 times more likely. The results presented here are for more than three days absent in the preceding month for eighth-grade students, but patterns for twelfth-grade students are similar, and the rates are about the same in 2005 as they were in 2000 (Hoffman and Llagas, 2003). Recent data on absenteeism were not available for California, so we present only national statistics.

### Enrollment in Preschool or Pre-K

Preschool attendance is believed to promote school readiness and has become the norm for four- and five-year-olds who have not yet entered kindergarten—almost 70 percent attended a center-based early childhood care and education program in 2005 (U.S. Department of Education, 2007a). This is one of the few indicators where African Americans rank higher than other groups. As shown in **Figure A.16**, in both the national and California comparisons, more African-American three- and four-year-olds attend preschool than whites. Latino children are about 1.4 times more likely to not attend preschool than white children. A notable difference in preschool attendance patterns across racial groups is that for whites and Latinos, non-poor students are much more likely to attend preschool, while for African-American students, non-poor and poor students are about equally likely to attend preschool.

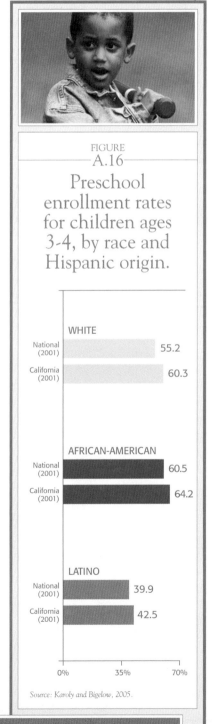

FIGURE
A.16

Preschool enrollment rates for children ages 3-4, by race and Hispanic origin.

WHITE

National (2001) — 55.2
California (2001) — 60.3

AFRICAN-AMERICAN

National (2001) — 60.5
California (2001) — 64.2

LATINO

National (2001) — 39.9
California (2001) — 42.5

0%    35%    70%

Source: Karoly and Bigelow, 2005.

# References

Amato, Paul R., "The Impact of Family Formation Change on the Cognitive, Social, and Emotional Well-Being of the Next Generation," *The Future of Children*, Vol. 15, No. 2, Autumn 2005, pp. 75–96.

Annie E. Casey Foundation, *KIDS COUNT Data Book: State Profiles of Child Well-Being*, Baltimore, Md., 2007.

Aquilino, William S., "The Life Course of Children Born to Unmarried Mothers: Childhood Living Arrangements and Young Adult Outcomes," *Journal of Marriage and the Family*, Vol. 58, No. 2, May 1996, pp. 293–310.

Aspen Institute Roundtable on Community Change, *Structural Racism and Community Building*, Washington, D.C., 2004.

Bailey, Amanda, and Joseph M. Hayes, "Who's in Prison? The Changing Demographics of Incarceration," in Hans P. Johnson, ed., *California Counts: Population Trends and Profiles*, Vol. 8, No. 1, San Francisco, Calif.: Public Policy Institute of California, August 2006.

Bhatia, Shashi K., and Subhash C. Bhatia, "Childhood and Adolescent Depression," *American Family Physician*, Vol. 75, No. 1, January 2007, pp. 73–80.

Bloom, B., and R. A. Cohen, "Summary Health Statistics for U.S. Children: National Health Interview Survey, 2006," *Vital and Health Statistics, Series 10*, No. 234, Hyattsville, Md.: National Center for Health Statistics, September 2007. As of July 1, 2008: http://www.cdc.gov/nchs/data/series/sr_10/sr10_234.pdf

Boer, Rob, Yuhui Zheng, Adrian Overton, Gregory K. Ridgeway, and Deborah A. Cohen, "Neighborhood Design and Walking Trips in Ten U.S. Metropolitan Areas," *American Journal of Preventive Medicine*, Vol. 32, No. 4, April 2007, pp. 298–304.

Bonczar, Thomas P., Prevalence of Imprisonment in the U.S. Population, 1974–2001, Washington, D.C: U.S. Department of Justice, Bureau of Justice Statistics Special Report, August 2003.

Bracht, Neil, "Prevention and Wellness," in R.L. Edwards, ed., *Encyclopedia of Social Work*, 19th Edition, Washington D.C.: National Association of Social Workers, 1995, pp. 1879–1886.

Brown, E. Richard, Shana A. Lavarreda, Ninez Ponce, Jean Yoon, Janet Cummings, and Thomas Rice, *The State of Health Insurance in California, Findings from the 2005 California Health Interview Report*, Los Angeles, Calif.: University of California, Los Angeles, Center for Health Policy Research, July 2007.

California Board of Corrections, *Repeat Offender Prevention Program: Final Report*, Sacramento, Calif., 2002.

California Department of Corrections and Rehabilitation, *California Prisoners and Parolees 2004: Summary Statistics on Adult Felon Prisoners and Parolees, Civil Narcotic Addicts and Outpatients and Other Populations*, Sacramento, Calif., 2005. As of July 1, 2008: http://www.cdcr.ca.gov/Reports_Research/Offender_Information_Services_Branch/Annual/CalPris/CALPRISd2004.pdf

————, Division of Juvenile Justice, *Department of Corrections and Rehabilitation Division of Juvenile Justice Population Overview as of December 31, 2007*, Sacramento, Calif., 2007a. As of July 1, 2008: http://www.cdcr.ca.gov/Reports_Research/research_tips.html

————, Expert Panel on Adult Offender and Recidivism Reduction Programming, *Report to the California State Legislature: A Roadmap for Effective Offender Programming in California*, Sacramento, Calif., 2007b.

————, Offender Information Services Branch, *Second and Third Striker Felons in the Adult Institution Population, December 31, 2007*, Sacramento, Calif., January 2008a.

———, **Offender Information Services Branch**, *Prison Census Data as of December 31, 2007*, Sacramento, Calif., February 2008b.

**California Department of Finance**, *2007 California Statistical Abstract*, Sacramento, Calif., January 2007a. As of July 1, 2008: http://www.dof.ca.gov/html/fs_data/stat-abs/statistical_abstract.php

**California Department of Finance**, *California Current Population Survey Report: March 2006*, Sacramento, Calif., September 2007b.

———, "Race/Ethnic Population with Age and Sex Detail," Web page, 2008, As of July 1, 2008: http://www.dof.ca.gov/HTML/DEMOGRAP/Data/DRUdatafiles.php

**California Department of Health Care Services**, "Firearm-Related Deaths by Race/Ethnicity, Age, and Sex, California, 2004," January 2007a. As of July 1, 2008: http://www.dhs.ca.gov/chs/OHIR/tables/datafiles/specificcauses/final%20firearms2001-2004.pdf

———, "Homicide Deaths by Race/Ethnicity, Age, and Sex, California, 2004," March 2007b. As of July 1, 2008: http://www.dhs.ca.gov/chs/OHIR/tables/datafiles/specificcauses/Homicide0004RaceAgeSex.pdf

———, "Infant Death Data Tables," Web page, 2007c. As of July 1, 2008: http://www.dhs.ca.gov/chs/ohir/tables/infant/childrace.htm

**California Department of Health Services**, *The Burden of Asthma in California: A Surveillance Report*, Sacramento, Calif., June 2007.

**California Department of Public Health**, *Sexually Transmitted Diseases in California, 2006*. Sacramento, Calif., November 2007a.

———, "Statewide Birth Statistical Tables," Web page, 2007b. As of July 1, 2008: http://ww2.cdph.ca.gov/data/statistics/Pages/StatewideBirthStatisticalDataTables.aspx

**California Health Interview Survey**. CHIS 2005 Adolescent Public Use File, Release 1 [computer file]. Los Angeles, Calif.: University of California, Los Angeles, Center for Health Policy Research, January 2007a.

———, CHIS 2005 Adult Public Use File, Release 1 [computer file], Los Angeles, Calif.: University of California, Los Angeles, Center for Health Policy Research, January 2007b.

**Carneiro, Pedro M., Costas Meghir,** and **Matthias Parey**, *Maternal Education, Home Environments and the Development of Children and Adolescents*, Bonn Germany: IZA, IZA Discussion Paper No. 3072, September 2007.

**Catalano, Shannon M.**, *Criminal Victimization, 2005*, Washington, D.C., U.S. Department of Justice, Bureau of Justice Statistics, NCJ 214644, September 2006. As of July 1, 2008: http://www.ojp.usdoj.gov/bjs/abstract/cv05.htm

———, *Criminal Victimization, 2006*. Washington, D.C., U.S. Department of Justice, Bureau of Justice Statistics, NCJ 219413, December 2007a. As of July 1, 2008: http://www.ojp.usdoj.gov/bjs/abstract/cv06.htm

———, "Intimate Partner Violence in the United States," U.S. Department of Justice, Bureau of Justice Statistics, Web page, 2007b. As of July 1, 2008: http://www.ojp.usdoj.gov/bjs/intimate/ipv.htm#contents

CDCR—*See* California Department of Corrections and Rehabilitation.

**Center for Substance Abuse Prevention**, *Community Partnerships: Promising Ways to Prevent Alcohol, Tobacco, and Other Drug Problems*, Washington, D.C.: U.S. Dept. of Health and Human Services, CSAP, 1995.

**Centers for Disease Control and Prevention**, "Cases of HIV infection and AIDS in the United States and Dependent Areas, 2005," *HIV/AIDS Surveillance Report*, Vol. 17, Revised Edition, Atlanta, Ga.: U.S. Department of Health and Human Services, Centers for Disease Control and Prevention, June 2007. As of July 1, 2008: http://www.cdc.gov/hiv/topics/surveillance/resources/reports/2005report/

———, "National Health Interview Survey, 2006," *Vital and Health Statistics*, Series 10, No. 236, Hyattsville, Md.: National Center for Health Statistics, January 2008. As of July 1, 2008: http://www.cdc.gov/nchs/data/series/sr_10/sr10_236.pdf

**Chaskin, Robert J., Selma Chipenda-Dansokho, Mark Joseph,** and **Carla Richards**, *An Evaluation of the Ford Foundation's Neighborhood and Family Initiative*, Chicago, Ill.: Chapin Hall Center for Children at the University of Chicago, 2001.

**Child Trends Databank**,weight Children and Youth," no date. As of July 1, 2008: http://www.childtrendsdatabank.org/indicators/15OverweightChildrenYouth.cfm

**Cohen, Deborah A., Sanae Inagami,** and **Brian Finch**, "The Built Environment and Collective Efficacy," *Health and Place*, Vol. 14, No. 2, June 2008, pp. 198–208.

**Cohen, Deborah, Amber Sehgal, Stephanie Williamson, Roland Sturm, Thomas L. McKenzie, Rosa Lara,** and **Nicole Lurie**, *Park Use and Physical Activity in a Sample of Public Parks in the City of Los Angeles.* Santa Monica, Calif.: RAND Corporation, TR-357-HLTH, 2006. As of July 1, 2008: http://www.rand.org/pubs/technical_reports/TR357/

**Cohen, Judith A.**, "Practice Parameters for the Assessment and Treatment of Children and Adolescents with Posttraumatic Stress Disorder," *Journal of the American Academy of Child and Adolescent Psychiatry*, Vol. 37, No. 10 Suppl., October 1998, pp. 4S–26S.

**Coleman, James S., E. Q. Campbell, C. J. Hobson, J. McPartland, A. M. Mood, F. D. Weinfeld,** and **R. L. York**, *Equality of Educational Opportunity.* Washington, D.C.: U.S. Department of Health, Education, and Welfare, Office of Education, 1966.

**Committee on Evaluation of Children's Health, National Research Council,** *Children's Health, the Nation's Wealth: Assessing and Improving Child Health*, Washington, D.C.: National Academies Press, 2004.

**County of Los Angeles Department of Health Services**, *HIV/AIDS Surveillance Summary*, HIV Epidemiology Program, Los Angeles, Calif., January 2005.

**Conley, D.,** and **N. G. Bennett**, "Race and the Inheritance of Low Birth Weight," *Social Biology*, Vol. 47, Nos. 1–2, Spring–Summer 2000, pp. 77–93.

**Cunradi, Carol B.**, "Drinking Level, Neighborhood Social Disorder, and Mutual Intimate Partner Violence," *Alcoholism: Clinical and Experimental Research.* Vol. 31, No. 6, June 2007, pp. 1012–1019.

**Currie, Jane,** and **Enrico Moretti**, "Mother's Education and the Intergenerational Transmission of Human Capital: Evidence from College Openings," *Quarterly Journal of Economics*, Vol. 118, No. 4, November 2003, pp. 1495–1532.

**Curtis, Nicola M., K. R. Ronan,** and **C. M. Borduin**, "Multisystemic Treatment: A Meta-Analysis of Outcome Studies," *Journal of Family Psychology*, Vol. 18, No. 3, 2004, pp. 411–419.

**Dellums Commission,** *A Way Out: Creating Partners for Our Nation's Prosperity by Expanding Life Paths of Young Men of Color*, Washington, D.C.: Joint Center for Political and Economic Studies, Health Policy Institute, 2006.

Desai, Sonalde, and Soumya Alva, "Maternal Education and Child Health: Is There a Strong Causal Relationship?," *Demography*, Vol. 35, No. 1, February 1998, pp. 71–81.

District of Columbia Department of Health, *The District of Columbia Healthy People 2010 Plan, A Strategy for Better Health*, September 2000. As of July 1, 2008: http://doh.dc.gov/doh/lib/doh/information/healthy_people2010/pdf/DC-HP2010-Plan.pdf

District of Columbia Department of the Environment, "DC's Air Pollution Days Have Declined by 44 Percent," news release, September 26, 2006. As of July 1, 2008: http://ddoe.dc.gov/ddoe/cwp/view,a,11,q, 494021,ddoeNav_GID,1458.asp

Do, D. Phuong, Tamara Dubowitz, Chloe E. Bird, Nicole Lurie, Jose J. Escarce, and Brian K. Finch, "Neighborhood Context and Ethnicity Differences in Body Mass Index: A Multilevel Analysis Using the NHANES III Survey (1988–1994)," *Economics and Human Biology*, Vol. 5, No. 2, July 2007, pp. 179–203.

Dubowitz, Tamara, Melonie Heron, Chloe E. Bird, Nicole Lurie, Brian K. Finch, Ricardo Basurto-Davila, Lauren Hale, and Jose J. Escarce, *Neighborhood Socioeconomic Status and Fruit and Vegetable Intake Among Whites, Blacks, and Mexican-Americans in the United States.* Santa Monica, Calif.: RAND Corporation, forthcoming.

Eaton, Danice K., Laura Kann, Steve Kinchen, James Ross, Joseph Hawkins, William A. Harris, Richard Lowry, Tim McManus, David Chyen, Shari Shanklin, Connie Lim, Jo Anne Grunbaum, and Howell Wechsler, "Youth Risk Behavior Surveillance—United States, 2005." *Morbidity and Mortality Weekly Report Surveillance Summaries*, Vol. 55, No. SS-5, June 9, 2006.

Edwards, Sharon L., and Renee F. Stern, *Building and Sustaining Community Partnerships for Teen Pregnancy Prevention: A Working Paper*, Cornerstone Consulting Group, Inc. Washington D.C.: Department of Health and Human Services, 1998.

English, Diana J., "The Extent and Consequences of Child Maltreatment," *The Future of Children.* Vol. 8, No. 1, Spring 1988, pp. 39–53.

Family Violence Prevention Fund, *Identifying and Responding to Domestic Violence: Recommendations for Child and Adolescent Health*, San Francisco, Calif., September 2002.

Federal Interagency Forum on Child and Family Statistics, *America's Children: Key National Indicators of Well-Being*, Washington, D.C. : U.S. Government Printing Office, 2007.

Finkelhor, David, Richard Ormrod, Heather Turner, and Sherry L. Hamby, "The Victimization of Children and Youth: A Comprehensive, National Survey," *Child Maltreatment*, Vol. 10, No. 1. February 2005, pp. 5–25.

Fiscella, Kevin, Peter Franks, Marthe R. Gold, and Carolyn M. Clancy, "Inequality in Quality: Addressing Socioeconomic, Racial, and Ethnic Disparities in Health Care," *Journal of the American Medical Association*, Vol. 283, No. 19, May 17, 2000, pp. 2579–2584.

Ford, Julie M., and Andrew A. Beveridge, "Neighborhood Crime Victimization, Drug Use, and Drug Sales: Results From the 'Fighting Back' Evaluation," *Journal of Drug Issues*, Vol. 36. No. 2, Spring 2006, pp. 393–416.

Fox, James A., and Marianna W. Zawitz, *Homicide Trends in the United States, Bureau of Justice Statistics*, Washington, D.C.: U.S. Department of Justice, Bureau of Justice Statistics, 2007. As of July 1, 2008: http://www.ojp.usdoj.gov/bjs/homicide/homtrnd.htm

Frank, Lawrence D., Martin A. Andresen, and Thomas L. Schmid, "Obesity Relationships with Community Design, Physical Activity, and Time Spent in Cars," *American Journal of Preventive Medicine*, Vol. 27, No. 2, August 2004, pp. 87–96.

**Franzini, Luisa, Jogn C. Ribble**, and **Arlene M. Keddie**, "Understanding the Hispanic Paradox," *Ethnicity and Disease*, Vol. 11, No. 3, October 2001, pp. 496–518.

**Freisthler, B. J.**, "Understanding the Spatial Relationship Between Child Maltreatment and Alcohol Outlet Density," *Dissertation Abstracts International, A: The Humanities and Social Sciences*, Vol. 64, No. 9, 2003, p. 3479-A.

**Freisthler, Bridget**, "A Spatial Analysis of Social Disorganization, Alcohol Access, and Rates of Child Maltreatment in Neighborhoods," *Children and Youth Services Review*, Vol. 26, No. 9, September 2004, pp. 803–819.

**Fryer, Roland G.**, and **Steven D. Levitt**, "Understanding the Black-White Test Score Gap in the First Two Years of School," *Review of Economics and Statistics*. Vol. 86, No. 2, May 2004, pp. 447–464.

**Furstenberg, Frank F.**, "Managing to Make It: Afterthoughts," *Journal of Family Issues*, Vol. 22, No. 2, 2001, pp. 150–162.

GAO—*See* U.S. Government Accountability Office.

**Gunier, Robert B., Andrew Hertz, Julie Von Behren**, and **Peggy Reynolds**, "Traffic Density In California: Socioeconomic and Ethnic Differences Among Potentially Exposed Children," *Journal of Exposure Analysis and Environmental Epidemiology*, Vol. 13, No. 3, 2003, pp. 240–246.

**Hack, Maureen, Nancy K. Klein**, and **H. Gerry Taylor**, "Long-Term Developmental Outcomes of Low Birth Weight Infants," *The Future of Children*, Vol. 5, No. 1, Spring 1995, pp. 176–196.

**Hallfors, Dennis D., Melinda Pankratz**, and **Shane Hartman**, "Does Federal Policy Support the Use of Scientific Evidence in School-Based Prevention Programs?" *Prevention Science*, Vol. 8, No. 1, March 2007, pp. 75–81.

**Hamilton, Brady E., Joyce A. Martin**, and **Stephanie J. Ventura**, "Births: Preliminary Data for 2006," *National Vital Statistics Reports*, Vol. 56, No. 7, Hyattsville, Md.: National Center for Health Statistics, December 5, 2007. As of July 1, 2008: http://origin.cdc.gov/nchs/data/nvsr/nvsr56/nvsr56_07.pdf

**Harrison, Paige M.**, and **Allen J. Beck**, *Prisoners in 2005*, Washington, D.C.: Department of Justice, Bureau of Justice Statistics, NCJ 215092, November 2006. As of July 1, 2008: http://www.ojp.usdoj.gov/bjs/abstract/p05.htm

**Hastert, Theresa A., Susan H. Babey, Allison L. Diamant**, and **E. Richard Brown**, *More California Teens Consume Soda and Fast Food Each Day Than Five Servings of Fruits and Vegetables*, Los Angeles, Calif.: University of California, Los Angeles, Center for Health Policy Research, September 2005.

**Hauser, Robert M., Brett V. Brown**, and **William R. Prosser**, eds., *Indicators of Children's Well-Being*. New York, N.Y.: Russell Sage Foundation, 1997.

**Hauser, Robert M., Devah I. Pager**, and **Solon J. Simmons**, "Race-ethnicity, Social Background, and Grade Retention," in Herbert J. Walberg, Arthur J. Reynolds, and Margaret C. Wang, eds., *Can Unlike Students Learn Together?: Grade Retention, Tracking, and Grouping*, Greenwich, Conn.: Information Age Publishing, 2004.

**Heckman, James J.**, *The Economics, Technology and Neuroscience of Human Capability Formation*, Cambridge, Mass.: National Bureau of Economic Research, Working Paper No. 13195, June 2007. As of July 1, 2008: http://www.nber.org/papers/w13195.

**Hennigan, Karen**, and **Kathy Kolnick**, *Juvenile Justice Data Project: A Partnership to Improve State and Local Outcomes—Summary Report: Phase I: Survey of Interventions and Programs*, Los Angeles, Calif.: Center for Research on Crime, University of Southern California, April 2007.

Hill, Robert B., *Synthesis of Research on Disproportionality in Child Welfare: An Update*. Seattle, Wa.: Casey Family Programs, 2006.

Hoffman, Kathryn, and Charmaine Llagas, "Status and Trends in the Education of Blacks," *Education Statistics Quarterly*, Vol. 5, No. 4, 2003.

Hofrichter, Richard, *Health and Social Justice: Politics, Ideology, and Inequity in the Distribution of Disease: A Public Health Reader*, San Francisco, Calif.: Jossey-Bass, 2003.

Holtby, Sue, Elaine Zahnd, Nicole Lordi, Christy McCain, Y. Jenny Chia, and John Kurata, *Health of California's Adults, Adolescents, and Children: Findings from CHIS 2003 and CHIS 2001*, Los Angeles, Calif.: University of California, Los Angeles, Center for Health Policy Research, May 2006.

Jaycox, Lisa H., Bradley D. Stein, Sheryl H. Kataoka, Marleen Wong, Arlene Fink, Pia Escudero, and Catalina Zaragoza, "Violence Exposure, Posttraumatic Stress Disorder, and Depressive Symptoms Among Recent Immigrant Schoolchildren," *Journal of the American Academy of Child and Adolescent Psychiatry*, Vol. 41, No. 9, September 2002, pp. 1104–1110.

Jimerson, Shane R., "On the Failure of Failure: Examining the Association Between Early Grade Retention and Education and Employment Outcomes During Late Adolescence," *Journal of School Psychology*, Vol. 37, No. 3, Autumn 1999, pp. 243–272.

Jones, Deborah J., Rex Forehand, Cara O'Connell, Lisa Armistead, and Gene Brody, "Mothers' Perceptions of Neighborhood Violence and Mother-Reported Monitoring of African-American Children: An Examination of the Moderating Role of Perceived Support," *Behavior Therapy*, Vol. 36, No. 1, Winter 2005, pp. 25–34.

Jonson-Reid, Melissa, and Richard P. Barth, "Maltreatment Report to Juvenile Incarceration: The Role Of Child Welfare Services," *Child Abuse and Neglect*, Vol. 24, No. 4, April 2000, pp. 505–520.

Karoly, Lynn A., and James H. Bigelow, The Economics of Investing in Universal Preschool Education in California, Santa Monica, Calif.: RAND Corporation, MG-349-PF, 2005. As of July 1, 2008: http://www.rand.org/pubs/monographs/MG349/

Karoly, Lynn A., M. Rebecca Kilburn, and Jill S. Cannon, *Early Childhood Interventions: Proven Results, Future Promise*. Santa Monica, Calif.: RAND Corporation, MG-341-PNC, 2005. As of July 1, 2008: http://www.rand.org/pubs/monographs/MG341/

Kelly, Michael P., Antony Morgan, Josiane Bonnefoy, Jennifer Butt, and Vivian Bergman, *The Social Determinants of Health: Developing an Evidence Base for Political Action—Final Report to World Health Organization Commission on the Social Determinants of Health*, October 2007.

Kidsdata.org, "Teen Births: Teen Birth Rate, by Race/Ethnicity: 2003," Web page, 2008. As of July 31, 2008: http://www.kidsdata.org/topictables.jsp?csid=0&t=17&i=2&ra=3_132&link=related

Kilburn, M. Rebecca, and Barbara L. Wolfe, "Resources Devoted to Child Development by Families and Society," in Neal Halfon, Kathryn Taaffe McLearn, and Mark A. Schuster, eds., *Child Rearing in America: Challenges Facing Parents with Young Children*. Cambridge, Mass.: Cambridge University Press, 2002.

Kilpatrick, Dean G., Kenneth J. Ruggiero, Ron Acierno, Benjamin E. Saunders, Heidi S. Resnick, and Connie L. Best, "Violence and Risk of PTSD, Major Depression, Substance Abuse/Dependence, and Comorbidity: Results from the National Survey of Adolescents," *Journal of Consulting and Clinical Psychology*, Vol. 71, No. 4, 2003, pp. 692–700.

King County Equity and Social Justice Initiative, *Working Toward Fairness and Opportunity for All*, Seattle, Wa., 2008.

Kirby, Douglas, Karin Coyle, and Jeffrey B. Gould, "Manifestations of Poverty and Birthrates Among Young Teenagers in California Zip Code Areas," *Family Planning Perspectives*, Vol. 33, No. 2, March–April 2001, pp. 63–69.

Komro, Kelli A., and Traci L. Toomey, "Strategies to Prevent Underage Drinking," *Alcohol Research and Health*, Vol. 26, No. 1, Winter 2002, pp. 5–14.

Krieger, N., D. L. Rowley, A. Herman, B. Avery, and M. T. Phillips, "Racism, Sexism, and Social Class: Implications for Studies of Health, Disease, and Well-Being," *American Journal of Preventive Medicine*, Vol. 9, No. 6 Supp., November–December 1993, pp. 82–122.

Kung, Hsiang-Ching, Donna L. Hoyert, Jiaquan Xu, and Sherry L. Murphy, *Infant Deaths and Infant Mortality Rates by Age, Sex, Race, and Hispanic Origin: United States, Final 2004 and Preliminary 2005*, Atlanta, Ga.: National Center for Health Statistics, Centers for Disease Control and Prevention, 2007. As of July 1, 2008: http://www.cdc.gov/nchs/products/pubs/pubd/hestats/prelimdeaths05/prelimdeaths05.htm

LaVeist, Thomas A., and John M. Wallace, Jr., "Health Risks and Inequitable Distribution of Liquor Stores in African-American Neighborhood," *Social Science and Medicine*, Vol. 51, No. 4, August 2000, pp. 613–617.

Lee, Helen, and Shannon McConville, "Death in the Golden State: Why Do Some Californians Live Longer?" in Hans P. Johnson, ed., *California Counts Population Trends and Profiles*, Vol. 9. No. 1, San Francisco, Calif.: Public Policy Institute of California, August 2007.

Legislative Analyst's Office, *A Primer: Three Strikes The Impact After More Than a Decade*, Sacramento, Calif., October 2005. As of July 1, 2008: http://www.lao.ca.gov/laoapp/PubDetails.aspx?id=1342

Legislative Analyst's Office, *California Justice System: A Primer*, Sacramento, Calif., January 31, 2007. As of July 1, 2008: http://www.lao.ca.gov/LAOApp/PubDetails.aspx?id=1543

Leibowitz, Arleen, "Parental Inputs and Children's Achievement," *Journal of Human Resources*, Vol. 12, No. 2, Spring 1977, pp. 242–251.

Leventhal, Tama, and Jeanne Brooks-Gunn, "The Neighborhoods They Live In: The Effects of Neighborhood Residence on Child and Adolescent Outcomes," *Psychological Bulletin*, Vol. 126, No. 2, March 2000, pp. 309–337.

———, "Diversity in Developmental Trajectories Across Adolescence: Neighborhood Influences," in Richard M. Lerner and Laurence Steinberg, eds., *Handbook of Adolescent Psychology, 2nd Edition*, New York, N.Y.: John Wiley & Sons, Inc., 2004.

Los Angeles County Children's Planning Council, *2006 Children's Scorecard*, Los Angeles, Calif., 2006. As of July 1, 2008: http://www.lapublichealth.org/childpc/resourcefiles/committees/cpc/cpc scorecard06.pdf

Los Angeles Urban League and The United Way, *The State of Black Los Angeles*, Los Angeles, Calif., July 2005.

Martin, Joyce A., Brady E. Hamilton, Paul D. Sutton, Stephanie J. Ventura, Fay Menacker, Sharon Kirmeyer, and Martha L. Munson, "Births: Final Data for 2005," *National Vital Statistics Reports*, Vol. 56, No. 6, Hyattsville, Md.: National Center for Health Statistics, December 5, 2007.

Mathews, T. J., Fay Menacker, and Marian F. MacDorman, "Infant Mortality Statistics from the 2000 Period Linked Birth/Infant Death Data Set," *National Vital Statistics Reports*, Vol. 50, No. 12, Hyattsville, Md.: National Center for Health Statistics, August 28, 2002.

Maynard, Rebecca A., *Kids Having Kids: A Robin Hood Foundation Special Report on the Costs of Adolescent Childbearing*, New York, N.Y.: Robin Hood Foundation, 1997.

Mayo Clinic, "Asthma," Web page, 2008. As of July 1, 2008: http://www.mayoclinic.com/health/asthma/AS99999

McLanahan, Sara, "Diverging Destinies: How Children Are Faring Under the Second Demographic Transition," *Demography*, Vol. 41, No. 4, November 2004, pp. 607–627.

Meng, Ying-Ying, Susan H. Babey, Theresa A. Hastert, and E. Richard Brown, *California's Racial and Ethnic Minorities More Adversely Affected by Asthma*, Los Angeles, Calif.: University of California, Los Angeles, Center for Health Policy Research, February 2007.

Moore, K. A., "Criteria for Indicators of Child Well-Being," in Robert M. Hauser, Brett V. Brown, and William R. Prosser, eds., *Indicators of Children's Well-Being*. New York, N.Y.: Russell Sage Foundation, 1997.

Moore, Latetia V., and Ana V. Diez Roux, "Associations of Neighborhood Characteristics with Location and Type of Food Stores," *American Journal of Public Health*, Vol. 96, No. 2, February 2006, pp. 325–331.

Moorman, Jeanne E., Rose Anne Rudd, Carol A. Johnson, Michael King, Patrick Minor, Cathy Bailey, Marissa R. Scalia, and Lara J. Akinbami, "National Surveillance for Asthma—United States, 1980–2004," *Morbidity and Mortality Weekly Report Surveillance Summaries*, Vol. 56, No. SS-8, October 19, 2007, pp. 1–14, 18–54.

Mulvaney-Day, Norah E., Margarita Alegria, and William Sribney, "Social Cohesion, Social Support, and Health Among Latinos in the United States," *Social Science and Medicine*, Vol. 64, No. 2, January 2007, pp. 477–495.

Mumola, Christopher J., *Incarcerated Parents and Their Children*, Washington, D.C.: U.S. Department of Justice, Bureau of Justice Statistics, NCJ 182335, August 2000. As of July 1, 2008: http://www.ojp.usdoj.gov/bjs/abstract/iptc.htm

Nanyonjo, Rebecca D., Susanne B. Montgomery, Naomi Modeste, and Edward Fujimoto, "A Secondary Analysis of Race/Ethnicity and Other Maternal Factors Affecting Adverse Birth Outcomes in San Bernardino County," *Maternal and Child Health Journal*, 2007.

National Center for Health Statistics, "Obesity Still a Major Problem New Data Show," news release, October 6, 2004. As of July 1, 2008: http://www.cdc.gov/nchs/pressroom/04facts/obesity.htm

———, "National Vital Statistics System," Web page, 2007. As of July 1, 2008: http://www.cdc.gov/nchs/nvss.htm

———, "Prevalence of Overweight Among Children and Adolescents: United States 2003–2004," Web page, 2007. As of July 1, 2008: http://www.cdc.gov/nchs/products/pubs/pubd/hestats/overweight/overwght_child_03.htm

National Center for Injury Prevention and Control, *Costs of Intimate Partner Violence Against Women in the United States*, Atlanta, Ga.: Centers for Disease Control and Prevention, 2003. As of July 1, 2008: http://www.cdc.gov/ncipc/pub-res/ipv_cost/ipv.htm

National Coalition for the Homeless, *How Many People Experience Homelessness?* Washington, D.C., 2007.

National Institute on Alcohol Abuse and Alcoholism, *Youth Drinking: Risk Factors and Consequences*, Bethesda, Md., Alcohol Alert No. 37, July 1997. As of July 1, 2008: http://pubs.niaaa.nih.gov/publications/aa37.htm

Newes-Adeyi, Gabriella, Chiung M. Chen, Gerald D. Williams, and Vivian B. Faden, *Trends in Underage Drinking in the United States, 1991–2005*, Bethesda, Md.: National Institute on Alcohol Abuse and Alcoholism, Surveillance Report No. 81, October 2007. As of July 1, 2008: http://pubs.niaaa.nih.gov/publications/surveillance81/Underage05.htm

Northridge, Mary E., Elliot D. Sclar, and Padmini Biswas, "Sorting Out the Connections Between the Built Environment and Health: A Conceptual Framework for Navigating Pathways and Planning Healthy Cities," *Journal of Urban Health*, Vol. 80, No. 4, December 2003, pp. 556–568.

Painter, Gary, and David I. Levine, "Family Structure and Youths' Outcomes: Which Correlations Are Causal?" *Journal of Human Resources*, Vol. 35, No. 3, Summer 2000, pp. 524–549.

Pearl, Michelle, Paula Braveman, and Barbara Abrams, "The Relationship of Neighborhood Socioeconomic Characteristics to Birthweight Among 5 Ethnic Groups in California," *American Journal of Public Health*, Vol. 91, No. 11, November 2001, pp. 1808–1114.

Peled, Einat, Peter G. Jaffe, and Jeffrey L. Edleson, *Ending the Cycle of Violence: Community Responses to Children of Battered Women.* Thousand Oaks, Calif.: Sage Publications, 1995.

Petersilia, Joan, *Understanding California Corrections*, Berkeley, Calif.: California Policy Research Center, University of California, May 2006.

Pew Center on the States, *One in 100: Behind Bars in America*, Washington, D.C., 2008.

Promising Practices Network, homepage, 2008a. As of July 1, 2008: http://www.promisingpractices.net/

———, "How Programs Are Considered," 2008b. As of July 1, 2008: http://www.promisingpractices.net/criteria.asp

———, "Programs That Work: Keepin' It Real (Refuse, Explain, Avoid, Leave)," Web page, 2008c. As of July 1, 2008: http://www.promisingpractices.net/program.asp?programid=200

———, "Programs That Work: Project ALERT," Web page, 2008d. As of July 1, 2008: http://www.promisingpractices.net/program.asp?programid=35

Public Policy Institute of California, *Just the Facts: Poverty in California*, San Francisco, Calif., November 2006. As of July 1, 2008: http://www.ppic.org/main/publication.asp?i=261

Ricketts, Sue A., Erin K. Murray, and Renee Schwalberg, "Reducing Low Birthweight by Resolving Risks: Results from Colorado's Prenatal Plus Program," *American Journal of Public Health*, Vol. 57, No. 11, November 2005, pp. 1952–1957.

Rodríguez, Michael A., Marlena Kane, Lupe Alonzo-Diaz, and George R. Flores, *One Out of Three Latino Adolescents Overweight or At Risk*, Los Angeles, Calif.: University of California, Los Angeles, Health Policy Fact Sheet, April 2005.

Russell, Steven T., Faye C. H. Lee, and the Latina/o Teen Pregnancy Prevention Workgroup, "Practitioners' Perspectives on Effective Practices for Hispanic Teenage Pregnancy Prevention," *Perspectives on Sexual and Reproductive Health*, Vol. 36, No. 4, July–August 2004, pp. 142–149.

Saenz, R., *The Growing Color Divide in U.S. Infant Mortality*, Washington, D.C.: Population Reference Bureau, October 2007.

Schiraldi, Vincent, Jason Colburn, and Eric Lotke, *Three Strikes and You're Out: An Examination of the Impact of Three Strike Laws 10 Years After Their Enactment*, Washington, D.C.: Justice Policy Institute, 2004. As of July 1, 2008: http://www.justicepolicy.org/images/upload/04-09_REP_ThreeStrikes Natl_AC.pdf

Scott, Molly M., Deborah A. Cohen, Kelly R. Evenson, John Elder, Diane Catellier, J. Scott Ashwood, and Adrian Overton, "Weekend Schoolyard Accessibility, Physical Activity, and Obesity: The Trial of Activity in Adolescent Girls (TAAG) Study," *Preventive Medicine*, Vol. 44, No. 5, May 2007, pp. 398–403.

Simmons, Charlene W., *Children of Incarcerated Parents*, Sacramento, Calif.: California Research Bureau, CRB Note Vol. 7, No. 2, March 2000.

Smith, James P., *The Impact of SES Over the Life-Course*. Santa Monica, Calif.: RAND Corporation, WR-318, 2005. As of July 1, 2008: http://www.rand.org/pubs/working_papers/WR318/

Snyder, Howard N., and Melissa Sickmund, M. (2006). *Juvenile Offenders and Victims: 2006 National Report*, Washington, D.C.: National Center for Juvenile Justice, March 2006. As of July 1, 2008: http://www.ojjdp.ncjrs.gov/ojstatbb/nr2006/index.html

Steele, C. Brooke, Lehida Meléndez-Morales, Richard Campoluci, Nickolas DeLuca, and Hazel D. Dean, *Health Disparities in HIV/AIDS, Viral Hepatitis, Sexually Transmitted Diseases, and Tuberculosis: Issues, Burden, and Response, A Retrospective Review, 2000–2004*. Atlanta, Ga.: Department of Health and Human Services, Centers for Disease Control and Prevention, November 2007.

Stiffman, A. R., E. Hadley-Ives, D. Elze, and S. Johnson, "Impact of Environment on Adolescent Mental Health and Behavior: Structural Equation Modeling," *American Journal of Orthopsychiatry*, Vol. 69, No. 1, 1999, pp. 73–86.

Stockman, Jamila K., Karen Garcia, Julie von Behren, Oliver Bembom, Nazerah Shaikh, and Richard Kreutzer, "Asthma Disparities Among African-Americans," *California Asthma Facts*, Vol. 2, No. 1, Sacramento, Calif.: Environmental Health Investigations Branch, California Department of Health Services, March 2004. As of July 1, 2008: http://www.ehib.org/paper.jsp?paper_key=Asthma_Disparities

Stone Soup Child Care Programs, "How We Work," Web page, no date. As of July 1, 2008: http://www.stonesoupchildcare.org/stonesoup/how_we_work.html#work

Sturm, Roland, "Disparities in the Food Environment Surrounding U.S. Middle and High Schools," *Public Health*, Vol. 122, No. 7, July 2008, pp. 681–690.

Travis, Jeremy, and Michelle Waul, "The Children and Families of Prisoners," in Jeremy Travis and Michelle Waul, eds., *Prisoners Once Removed: The Impact of Incarceration and Reentry on Children, Families, and Communities*, Washington, D.C.: The Urban Institute Press, Washington, 2003.

Travis, Jeremy, Elizabeth Cincotta McBride, and Amy L. Solomon, *Families Left Behind: The Hidden Costs of Incarceration and Reentry*. Washington, D.C.: The Urban Institute Justice Policy Center, Policy Brief, June 2005.

U.S. Census Bureau, "American Community Survey, 2006," Web page, 2006. As of July 1, 2008: http://www.census.gov/acs/www/index.html

———, *The 2008 Statistical Abstract: The National Data Book*, Washington, D.C., 2008. As of July 1, 2008: http://www.census.gov/compendia/statab/

U.S. Department of Education, National Center for Education Statistics, *The Condition of Education 2007*, Washington, D.C., 2007a.

———, *Digest of Education Statistics: 2007*, 2007b. As of July 1, 2007: http://nces.ed.gov/programs/digest/d07/

———, *The Nation's Report Card: Reading 2007—National Assessment of Educational Progress at Grades 4 and 8*, Washington, D.C., NCES 2007-496, 2007c.

**U.S. Department of Health and Human Services**, *Youth and Tobacco: Preventing Tobacco Use Among Young People*, A Report of the Surgeon General, Washington, D.C., 1994. As of July 1, 2008: http://www.cdc.gov/tobacco/data_statistics/sgr/sgr_1994/index.htm

———, *Mental Health: A Report of the Surgeon General*, Rockville, Md.: National Institute of Mental Health. Rockville, 1999. As of July 1, 2008: http://www.surgeongeneral.gov/library/mentalhealth/home.html

———, Administration on Children, Youth, and Families, *Child Maltreatment 2005*. Washington, D.C.: U.S. Government Printing Office, 2007.

**U.S. Department of Justice, Bureau of Justice Statistics**, "Survey of Inmates in State and Federal Correctional Facilities, 2004" [computer file]. ICPSR04572-v1. Ann Arbor, Mich.: Inter-University Consortium for Political and Social Research [producer and distributor], February 28, 2007.

———, "Crime: State Level: State-by-State and National Trends," Web page, 2008. As of July 1, 2008: http://bjsdata.ojp.usdoj.gov/dataonline/Search/Crime/State/StatebyState.cfm.

**U.S. Department of Labor, Bureau of Labor Statistics**, "Local Area Unemployment Statistics: Employment Status of the Civilian Noninstitutional Population in States by Sex, Race, Hispanic or Latino ethnicity, Marital Status, and Detailed Age: 2004 Annual Averages," 2004. As of July 1, 2008: http://www.bls.gov/lau/table14full04.pdf

———, "Employment and Earnings: Tables Created by BLS: Tables from Employment and Earnings: Annual Average Data," 2008. As of July 1, 2008: http://www.bls.gov/cps/cpsa2007.pdf. Viewed March 6, 2008.

**U.S. Government Accountability Office**. (2007). *African-American Children in Foster Care: Additional HHS Assistance Needed to Help States Reduce the Proportion in Care*, Washington D.C., GAO-07-816, July 2007.

**U.S. Conference of Mayors**, *Hunger and Homelessness Survey: A Status Report on Hunger and Homelessness in America's Cities*. Washington, D.C., December 2006.

**Wehlage, Gary G., R. Rutter, Gregory A. Smith, N. Lesko**, and **R. Fernandez**, *Reducing the Risk: Schools as Communities of Support*, New York: Falmer Press, 1989.

**Wells, William**, and **William DeLeon-Granados**, "Intimate Partner Homicide in California, 1987–2000" [computer file]. ICPSR version. Carbondale, Ill.: Southern Illinois University [producer], 2002. Ann Arbor, Mich.: Inter-University Consortium for Political and Social Research [distributor], 2003.

**Western, Bruce**, *Punishment and Inequality in America*, New York: Russell Sage Foundation, 2006.

**Williams, David R.**, and **Chiquita Collins**, "U.S. Socioeconomic and Racial Differences in Health: Patterns and Explanations," *Annual Review of Sociology*, Vol. 21, August 1995, pp. 349–386.

**Wilson, Nance, Leonard Syme, Thomas Boyce, Victor A. Battistich**, and **Steve Selvin**, "Adolescent Alcohol, Tobacco, and Marijuana Use: The Influence of Neighborhood Disorder and Hope,"*American Journal of Health Promotion*, Volume 20, No. 1, September 2005, pp. 11–19.

**Wise, Paul H.**, "The Anatomy of a Disparity in Infant Mortality," *Annual Review of Public Health*, Vol. 24, 2003, pp. 341–362.